Smoke Signals

The Native Takeback of North America's Tobacco Industry

Jim Poling, Sr.

DUNDURN
TORONTO

Project Editor: Michael Carroll
Editor: Dominic Farrell
Design: Jennifer Scott
Printer: Webcom

Library and Archives Canada Cataloguing in Publication

Poling, Jim (Jim R.)

    Smoke signals : the native takeback of North America's tobacco industry / Jim Poling Sr.

Includes bibliographical references and index.
Issued also in electronic format.
ISBN 978-1-4597-0640-8

1. Indians of North America--Tobacco use. 2. Indians of North America--Medicine. 3. Tobacco use--Health aspects--North America--History. 4. Tobacco industry--Government policy--North America. I. Title.

E98.T6P65 2012   394.1'408997   C2012-903222-0

1   2   3   4   5   16   15   14   13   12

 Conseil des Arts du Canada   Canada Council for the Arts   Canada    ONTARIO ARTS COUNCIL CONSEIL DES ARTS DE L'ONTARIO

We acknowledge the support of the **Canada Council for the Arts** and the **Ontario Arts Council** for our publishing program. We also acknowledge the financial support of the **Government of Canada** through the **Canada Book Fund** and **Livres Canada Books**, and the **Government of Ontario** through the **Ontario Book Publishing Tax Credit** and the **Ontario Media Development Corporation**.

Printed and bound in Canada.

Visit us at
Dundurn.com
Definingcanada.ca
@dundurnpress
Facebook.com/dundurnpress

Dundurn	Gazelle Book Services Limited	Dundurn
3 Church Street, Suite 500	White Cross Mills	2250 Military Road
Toronto, Ontario, Canada	High Town, Lancaster, England	Tonawanda, NY
M5E 1M2	LA1 4XS	U.S.A. 14150

This book is dedicated to the memory of Billy,
an Anishnabek youth who lost hope and took his life
many years ago in northwestern Ontario.
No one should ever die young because of hope lost.

Contents

Hail thou inspiring plant! Thou balm of life,
Well might thy worth engage two nations' strife;
Exhaustless fountain of Britannia's wealth;
Thou friend of wisdom and thou source of health.

— From an Early Tobacco Label

Introduction

Writings about tobacco cascade from cliffs of books, magazine articles, research papers, and government studies. Think of any place where words exist and tobacco is there; it is surely one of the world's most thought about and written about topics. There have been billions of words, perhaps trillions, written about this one plant in the five hundred years since it was introduced to Europeans — who at the time were ravenous for gold, not botanical curiosities.

Columbus mentioned it in his diary after landing in the West Indies while trying to find his way to the Orient. Jacques Cartier, who landed farther north than Columbus, in what is now Canada, also wrote about this odd weed, unknown in Europe but chewed, smoked, and used as medicine by the Indians. The first quill strokes that these explorers put to paper about the New World gave the plant scant attention, but the world soon became obsessed with it.

Today, do an Internet search for *tobacco* and you get 160 million hits in 0.12 seconds. Try *smoking* and you get five hundred million hits in 0.16 seconds. *Tobacco control* produces 24 million hits in 0.18 seconds.

Many world governments now are awash with policies, reports, conferences, and visioning sessions on tobacco and the problems tobacco has created for humankind, plus the economic benefits gained through tobacco taxation. Tobacco control has become an industry, growing ever larger as anti-smoking campaigns target developing countries.

If few subjects have been more written about in the history of the world, why then would anyone write yet another word about tobacco, let alone another book? Well, the reason is exactly because so much has been written already. Few people have the time, or the inclination, to read everything about tobacco, so it seemed like a good idea to gather the most interesting and pertinent pieces of tobacco history and combine them with information about the developments and issues of today, including contraband and smuggling.

Smoke Signals is not in any way an academic study. It is an attempt to help readers become more informed about an issue that has much impact, direct and indirect, on their lives. We live in a society in which information is spilling over the gunwales of our daily lives, swamping us before we can become properly informed. An informed public is critical, however, in helping governments make the best decisions for solving the social and economic problems arising from tobacco and its related issues.

Tobacco is an especially difficult and complex subject, especially in North America, because Natives are inexorably connected to it. They introduced European settlers to tobacco, and now are taking back control of more and more of the aspects of the growth, processing, distribution, and selling of it. The issues of tobacco use and the unresolved grievances of Native people need to be discussed and resolved together.

A note on terminology: It is difficult to know what to call the original inhabitants of the Americas without offending someone. The term *Indian* is a misnomer created by Europeans who thought they had found the Far East when they landed in North America. It is a term not liked by some people, some Natives included.

In the 1970s the politically correct name for Canada's Native citizens living on reserves became "First Nations" people. The name does not cover all original peoples, however. There are Métis and Inuit, neither of whom live on reserves, and many Natives do not live on reserves and are not covered by the First Nations terminology.

The Canadian federal government now uses the term *Aboriginal* to cover all varieties of Natives that it used to refer to as Indians. In North America, however, the word *Aboriginal* always had been thought of in relation to Australia and its aborigines. *Aboriginal* is a term abhorred by some people because it never applied to North America in the first place. Also, it is seen as a way in which governments can lump all Natives together, without distinguishing them as separate peoples who form different Native nations.

In the United States, *Indian* is still the preferred word for Natives. Another distinction exists in the terminology used in the two nations: in the United States there are reservations, whereas in Canada there are reserves.

This book tries to call Native people what they call themselves: Anishnabek, Mohawk, Puyallup, Mi'kmaq, et cetera. When specific names cannot be used, I prefer *Native* rather than *Aboriginal* or *Indian*. However, for U.S. references, the term *Indian* is used when a specific name cannot be used, since that is the term in use in that country; *Indian* is also used for all Canadian historical references when more than one tribe or nation is addressed because that's how they were known until relatively recent times.

A note on the use of statistics. "There are three kinds of lies: lies, damned lies, and statistics." This witty truth was popularized by Mark Twain (although it was not created by the great American writer). Whoever created it was trying to show the persuasive power of numbers, particularly the use of statistics to embroider and exaggerate an argument. In the tobacco control industry, statistics are sprinkled generously to flavour anti-smoking messages.

They vary from organization to organization and they are often reasonably accurate, but no one should accept them without further investigation. The same applies to government statistics, and spending and revenue numbers.

Numbers are like fresh pretzel dough; they can be twisted into any form that suits the imagination, and should not be accepted at first glance.

1

Gift of the Manitou

No one knows exactly when it all began, but it was sometime after the last ice age, perhaps eight thousand years ago, give or take a few millennia. Melting and withdrawing ice released frozen soils, exposing them to the warming sun, and encouraging plant life to awaken and flourish. More warmth brought more plant life as the great glaciers diminished.

After the ice withdrew, the mammoths, mastodons, and other huge beasts that had fed early humans disappeared rapidly, and inexplicably. It is believed that 85 percent of the earth's large mammals became extinct at this time. No one knows exactly why, but the substantial climate change had to have been a factor.

The dramatic loss of the megafauna changed human life. Man, the hunter, was confronted with a dwindling source of once plentiful meat, and had to seek other sources of food. Legumes, more plentiful in the newly freed soils, were found to fill bellies and offer variety. People gathered more legumes as more big animals disappeared, and a natural progression saw them experimenting with the cultivation of plants for consumption. They learned methods of collecting seeds, planting them, and tricks for nurturing them into crops that produced valuable foods.

In the South American Andes, early Amerindians became experts at cultivating plants in a region with climate zones ranging from coastal deserts to tropical jungles to soaring mountain peaks. They tested many wild plants, making remarkable discoveries that gave the world the potato, the tomato, and the chili pepper — all members of the strange nightshade family. There are 1,700 species of nightshade, many of them tasty, desirable additions to the human diet. Others are toxic to the point of being poisonous. Experimentation brought some tragedies, no doubt — all part of the learning process — but there were also many valuable successes.

The early peoples developed advanced agriculture practices, including the art of terracing hillsides and the use of organic fertilizers. More than one-half of the foods consumed in the world today were developed or cultivated in the Andes. The Incas and the Aztecs, who occupied what is now Mexico, created the only true empires existing in the Americas when the first Europeans arrived. and developed agricultural practices that were considered more advanced than those of the Spanish who conquered them.

One member of the Andes nightshade family was a tall, thick-stemmed plant with oily, hairy leaves. Early Andean peoples sniffed it, rubbed it on their skins, boiled it, and chewed it. They did not eat it, though; instead, they spat it out after chewing it, not liking its bitter, unpalatable taste. As a food they found it useless, but as a medicine it had possibilities. It became known as tobacco.

Its juices made an effective insecticide to keep bugs away, and the Amerindians found that it could be used as a medicine: it could be rubbed on a wound, or placed in the mouth to soothe toothache, a common ailment before dentistry. Tobacco leaves boiled in water produced a hallucinogenic drink, which the Amerindians believed brought them closer to their spirits. This was a critical discovery. It became valued as a bridge between their two worlds: their own physical world, and the supernatural world of the spirits who controlled their lives.

How tobacco first came to be smoked is anyone's guess. Perhaps some early people were sitting around a campfire when someone tossed an armful of brush containing a wild tobacco plant onto the fire. Those sitting downwind inhaled the smoke and almost immediately felt their mood change. They discovered that tobacco smoke taken into the body can act as both a stimulant and a relaxant, depending on the dosage. The mood alteration the Amerindians experienced when using tobacco came from an ingredient later named *nicotine*, which was found in much stronger concentrations in Amerindian tobacco than that of later commercial tobaccos. Some researchers suggest that the wild tobacco cultivated by the early Amerindians contained ten times more nicotine than the tobacco grown commercially today.

It is known that when they began cultivating wild tobacco, the early Amerindians found they could encourage better next-season growth if they burned old, standing plants in the autumn. They would have discovered very early that inhaling smoke from these fires could be intoxicating. Wild tobacco smoke, inhaled deeply, produced mind alterations that ranged from a mild and pleasant relaxation to outright hallucinations.

So, even though they couldn't eat it, the Amerindians of the Andes began cultivating tobacco for use as a medicine, as an insecticide, and for achieving spiritual highs. They could not know it at the time, but they were the only possessors of this odd plant because it was native only to the Americas. Sole possession did not last long, however, as tobacco seeds and tobacco spread via hunting parties, trade, and other wanderings. It took centuries for tobacco seeds to spread from tribe to tribe, but it eventually travelled into the Amazon and Argentina, and north through Central America into most of North America.

By the time the first European explorers were setting sail on the Atlantic, tobacco was an essential part of life among the diverse

Amerindian populations scattered through the vastness of the Americas. Almost all Amerindians used tobacco as a medicine, and as a way of connecting themselves with the spirit world.

Despite the differences in Amerindian languages and cultures, Native beliefs about tobacco and its uses are remarkably similar. Almost all believe it to be a sacred gift from the gods. It bridges the natural and supernatural, and offering tobacco to the spirits is an important way to maintain good relations between those two worlds.

Tobacco is at the centre of many tribal creation stories, an indication of just how long Indians have been using the plant. The Navajo believe that the universe could not be created until Sky Father and Earth Mother had smoked sacred tobacco. The Iroquois of the Great Lakes region believe that tobacco was given to them as a means of communicating with the spiritual world. Burning tobacco creates sacred smoke that lifts their praise and petitions to Ha-wen-neyu, the Great Spirit. The Aztecs, although their spirits demanded human blood, used smoke to carry blood gifts up to them.

The Winnebego of southern Lake Michigan tell of how their Earthmaker created spirits who lived above and below the earth, and in the water, and how he gave them powers over certain things in the world. Later he created humans, but gave them no powers over anything, except a special weed. The spirits were not given the weed and they had no power to take it away from humans. The spirits craved the tobacco but could not get it, so when humans needed something, they offered tobacco to the spirits, asking them to take pity and to grant them their blessings.

The Anishnabek, who include the Ojibwe and Chippewa, are encouraged to carry *asemaa*, tobacco, with them at all times to give thanks and to ask for special help. According to Eugene Goodsky, a Chippewa elder from Bois Forte, Minnesota, "Praying without asemaa is like talking on the telephone with the cord unplugged."

Tobacco was a part of everyday Native life throughout the ancient Americas. Its smoke was a cleansing and healing agent. It was used not only to help the physically ill but to promote good thoughts at social and ritualistic occasions. When people smoked together at important meetings, they were calling on the spirits to witness their words and promises. No ceremonies among the Algonquian tribes of eastern Canada could be held without tobacco.

Anthropologist Ralph Linton notes in his research on Indian use of tobacco: "As a sacrifice it might be burned as incense, cast into the air or on the ground, or buried. There were sacred places at which every visitor left a tobacco offering, and during storms it was thrown into lakes and rivers to appease the under-water powers. Smoking was indulged in on all solemn occasions, such as councils, and was a necessary part of most religious ceremonies."

Historically, there were different levels of tobacco use. Generally, Indian populations used tobacco in ceremonies around sacred items. It also was used at closed meetings of secret societies, such as medicine societies. Tobacco's mind-altering properties allowed shamans, or other spiritual leaders, to have visions in which they travelled into spiritual worlds.

Tobacco was not the only mind-altering substance used by Indians in the Americas. There were also such things as peyote, mescal, datura, and a variety of hallucinogenic mushrooms. Tobacco, however, was the most widely used substance in ceremonies and rituals, possibly because its effects were not as harsh, nor as long-lasting. A shaman could achieve a quick high by ingesting tobacco, but return quickly to normal.

Natives knew the power of tobacco to affect the mind. They also would have known its addictive traits, its potential to create the craving for more. The subject of tobacco addiction among early Indians is a controversial one, however, since it involves the conflict between the sacredness of tobacco and its recreational use.

Unlike alcohol, a recreational drug that was introduced to Indians by foreigners, tobacco was indigenous and its use had spiritual origins and specific purposes. It was a sacred gift for ceremonies and rituals designed to secure peace and friendship, and to solemnize vows and petitions to the spirits. It also was a shamanistic tool.

Tobacco's nicotine is highly addictive, however, and some Indians who smoked it likely became hooked on it, and did use it just because their bodies demanded it. Medical evidence of how tobacco smoke affects the human body supports a view that there must have been some addiction among early Indian populations. Modern research has shown that after only one use, the probability of dependence on tobacco is 32 percent. Still, there is scant evidence of wide-scale addiction among general Indian populations, at least on the scale that we have seen in modern societies.

The *Encyclopedia of Psychoactive Substances* gives this opinion: "In recognition of its awesome properties, Native Americans traditionally restricted their use of tobacco by smoking only in the context of sacred ceremonies." There is evidence, however, of recreational use of tobacco in some Amerindian societies. The Aztecs, for example, smoked after feasts to aid digestion.

There is corroborating testimony about the regular recreational use among tribes from early explorers and missionaries. *Relations des jésuites*, the extensive reports made by the Jesuit missionaries in Canada, contain references to Indians smoking. One writer notes observing Indians with "small pouches in which they carry the tobacco which they smoke perpetually, at the assemblies, and everywhere."

Another, Paul Le Jeune, a Jesuit superior from Quebec, reported in 1634 on the tobacco use of the Montagnais: "The fondness they have for this herb is beyond all belief. They go to sleep with the reed pipes in their mouths, they sometimes get up in the night to smoke; they often stop in their journeys for the same purpose, and it is the first thing they do when they re-enter their cabins. I have lighted tinder, so as to allow them to smoke while paddling a canoe; I have often seen them gnaw at the stems of pipes when they have no more tobacco. I have seen them scrape and pulverize a wooden pipe to smoke it. Let us say with compassion that they pass their lives in smoke, and at death fall into the fire."

Le Jeune may have looked unfavourably on the tobacco addiction he witnessed amongst the Indians, but he also made an astute observation about one of the positive aspects of tobacco: It was used by the Indians to suppress hunger. Hunger suppression and pain abatement quickly became two prominent reasons for tobacco use, notably among soldiers and sailors.

The bond between hunger and tobacco use was also mentioned by Henry Schoolcraft, an Indian agent in Michigan in the 1820s: "Under all their sufferings, the pipe of the hunter is his chief solace, and a solace often resorted to. Smoking parties are frequently formed, when there is a scarcity of food not tending, as might be supposed, to destroy social feeling and render the temper sour. On these occasions the entertainer sends a message to this effect: 'Come and smoke with me. I have no food; but we can pass away the evening very well without it.'"

So, it is likely that some early Indians were addicted to tobacco, but the spiritual value of the plant, plus its limited availability, prevented the widespread addiction seen in later times. Tobacco supplies were limited by the time it took to cultivate and prepare it for use, time and tools needed for gathering, hunting, fishing, growing, and the many other things people living off the land needed to survive. Also, when a tobacco supply was exhausted, there were no convenience stores to visit for restocking. Many such factors created long periods when tobacco was not available for recreational smoking.

The Indian relationship with tobacco would change, though, after Caribbean Indians spotted the first European sail on the

Atlantic horizon. When the strange people from across the ocean came ashore, it was natural for the Amerindians to present these God-like beings with tobacco leaves. Tobacco was a sacred gift, offering respect, friendship, and peace. It was a symbol of good faith and good relations, but the Europeans missed the symbolism and dismissed the Indians as prehistoric "savages."

The explorers from the Old World felt that they did not need the respect of these uncivilized people, nor would they give respect to Indian culture, which they viewed as pagan and barbaric. That first gift of tobacco was not appreciated and not accepted, but in the end, the Europeans were entranced by tobacco and it soon became a curse that would affect the entire world.

2

Pandora's Box

Christopher Columbus was not impressed with the welcoming offerings of the indigenous Arawaks when he landed in the New World in October 1492. With outstretched arms, the Indians presented him with fruits and large dried leaves that "gave of a distinct fragrance."

One can't blame the admiral for not being excited over gifts of fruit and dried leaves. He was looking for Cathay, where he expected to find silk, spices, silver and gold, and other riches. So, when the first meeting between inhabitants of Europe and the Americas ended, Columbus returned to his ship and told his men to toss the worthless dried leaves overboard. He didn't bother to describe the leaves in detail, nor did the two crew members who, more than three weeks later, saw Indians smoking leaves on the island of Cuba.

Columbus and his men could not have known the impact of those tobacco leaves on the world over the next five hundred years. However, nothing that they could have found in Cathay could have had anywhere near the life-altering impacts of those worthless-looking leaves.

Even the Spaniards who immediately followed Columbus little noted the leaves, and the Indians' use of them. Hernán Cortés, conqueror of Mexico and annihilator of the Aztecs, did observe that the Aztec emperor, Montezuma, smoked leaves after dinner. And, Francisco Orellana, the conquistador who played a part in the destruction of the Inca empire, described Amazon Indians blowing smoke at intruders in a form of assault sorcery. But none of the first Spanish conquistadors described tobacco in detail, or how and why the Indians used it.

A Spanish priest, Bartolome' de las Casas, wrote briefly about the first encounter with tobacco smoking in his 1527 book, *Historia de las Indias*. Drawing on Columbus's journal, he wrote that two crew members, Luis de Torres and Rodrigo de Jerez, were the first Europeans to encounter tobacco smoking, which they witnessed when they went ashore on one of the Caribbean islands: "These two Christians met many people on the road, men and women, and the men always with a firebrand in their hands, and certain herbs to take their smokes, which are some dry herbs put in a certain leaf, dry also, after the fashion of a musket made of paper, such as boys make on the feast of the Holy Ghost. These are lit at one end, and at the other they chew or suck and take in with their breath that smoke which dulls their flesh and as it were intoxicates and so they say that they do not feel weariness. Those muskets, or whatever we call them, they call *tobacos*."

The French, during their discoveries of Canada, were more observant. Jacques Cartier, on his finding of Hochelaga (Montreal) in October 1535, observed and noted the strange and previously unknown practice of smoking leaves:

> They have a grass (plant) of which they gather a large quantity for the winter's use, which is held in great favor and used by the men only and in the following manner: They dry it in the sun and carry it in a little pouch of skin around their necks, with a horn (cornet) of stone or wood (a pipe); they make this grass into

powder and put it into one of the ends of the horn, then place a hot coal on the top of it and suck at the other end, filling their bodies with smoke so that it comes out from their mouths and nostrils like from the pipe of a chimney; they say this keeps them healthy and warm, and they never go anywhere without having these articles. We tried this smoking, putting some of the smoke in our mouths, which was as hot as pepper.

Decades later Samuel de Champlain wrote about the significance of tobacco for important occasions amongst the Indians that he encountered, and about the spiritual connections of tobacco smoke for them. In May 1603 he visited Tadoussac, a Montagnais village at the confluence of the Saguenay and St. Lawrence Rivers. He described a meeting in which a "savage," who had been brought to France to show to the king, told of his visit to that strange world across the water. One of the main listeners was the grand chief Anadabijou.

"He was heard with the greatest possible silence. Now when he had ended his oration, the said grand Sagamore Anadabijou, who had listened to him attentively, began to smoke tobacco, and to pass on his pipe to Monsieur du Pont-Gravé of St. Malo, and to me, and to certain other Sagamores who were near him. After smoking some time, he began to address the whole gathering, speaking with gravity, pausing sometimes a little, and then resuming his speech...."

Ten years later Champlain was travelling west from Montreal when he met fifteen canoes of Algonquin at the Chutes de la Chaudière (rapids that run through downtown Ottawa) on the Ottawa River. The rapids were about sixty metres wide and dropped fifteen metres over a short distance, so they had to be portaged. Champlain observed the Indians taking tobacco, placing it on a birch bark piece and dancing and singing around it. After making a speech to the waterfall, one of the Indians threw the tobacco into the whirlpool at the base of the rapids.

Thomas Hariot, a member of England's first colonization attempt in the Chesapeake Bay region, had reported seeing similar use of tobacco, or *uppowoc*.

"Sometimes they make holy fires and cast the powder into them as a sacrifice. If there is a storm on the waters, they throw it up into the air and into the water to pacify their gods. Also, when they set up a new weir for fish, they pour uppowoc into it. And if they escape from danger, they also throw the powder up into the air. This is always done with strange gestures and stamping, sometimes dancing, clapping of hands, holding hands up, and staring up into the heavens. During this performance they chatter strange words and utter meaningless noises."

The tobacco was a gift to the spirits in return for safe passage. That was the message the Indians tried to present to Columbus and others who arrived after him. Tobacco was a gift of friendship and respect, but the Europeans were too distracted by material things to grasp the spiritual message.

Although Cartier and others who tried smoking tobacco found it a foul experience, others experienced pleasure and took to it quickly. Rodrigo de Jerez, one of the two men who saw Indians smoking during the first Columbus voyage, tried it, was hooked, and became a regular smoker. When he returned home to Spain, he brought tobacco and showed his fellow villagers how the smoke could be inhaled, then expelled. The sight of smoke pouring from his mouth frightened them, and de Jerez was arrested and thrown into prison for seven years by the Inquisition. His accusers ruled that smoking was sinful, and that only the Devil himself had the power to pour smoke from his mouth.

Many of the Spanish explorers and colonizers reviled and denounced the inhaling of tobacco smoke, yet others who tried it often found they wanted more. The high nicotine content of the Indian tobacco made it compelling and pulled some into addiction.

Mystifying as it was to many Europeans, tobacco use spread. Those who disapproved of it had no idea what purpose smoking served — the spiritual role that tobacco served for the Indians was beyond their comprehension — nor did they have any conception of the addictive powers of tobacco, or its dangers. For most Europeans at the time, the inhaling of smoke was clearly the work of the Master of Hell. Yet, some began to understand that tobacco as a commodity had commercial possibilities, and when they did, they opened a Pandora's box.

Tobacco has little spiritual value in today's world, but is a major reason for some of the world's most serious social problems. The World Health Organization (WHO) says that tobacco use kills about six million people a year and causes hundreds of billions of dollars of economic damage. Tobacco smuggling funds terrorist and organized crime groups, and is used as a means of laundering money for drug cartels. Law-enforcement agencies say that cigarette diversion deprives world governments of $50 billion a year.

The human grief caused by tobacco over five centuries might be seen by some as just revenge for European savagery against the Natives of the Americas. Spanish conquistadors like Cortes, Orellana, and Francisco Pizarro, the man who destroyed the Incan Empire, treated the Amerindians as sub-human animals. They took their minerals, their riches, and their women, while shattering their cultures and beliefs. In return they left them trinkets and diseases — and, in the case of the Spanish, the horse.

The gift of tobacco leaves that those early Amerindians gave to the world with welcoming, outstretched arms has produced a hellish legacy. The newcomers to the Americas took the simple native tobacco leaf, cultivated it, experimented with it, became addicted to it, and created an industry that today turns out 5.7

trillion cigarettes a year, employs two million people, and creates significant wealth for governments. It also generates a product that causes deadly health problems, and social evils.

The Europeans took the leaf, but threw away the Indian understanding of tobacco. They were intrigued with its possible medicinal uses, lured and trapped by its nicotine, then addicted to the comforts it offered and the money that it produced. They forgot, or ignored, the Indian belief that tobacco was a sacred plant linked to the spiritual world.

The recreational tobacco use rampant throughout the world today is also epidemic in Native populations, but traditional Native teachings about tobacco use have not been lost completely. Tobacco is still used in Native rituals, and today is an important part of teachings designed to revive and strengthen Native culture and traditions. In these rituals, the core belief about tobacco remains what it was in the beginning: an offering to the spiritual world. A bond between the giver and the receiver.

Many Native elders, and others who retain traditional Native beliefs, teach that recreational tobacco use is disrespectful to the traditional spiritual and medicinal uses. There are attempts in Native communities to restore the original understanding of tobacco. While this can be seen as a positive development, it can also be argued that the special status afforded to tobacco in Native societies also weakens support for tobacco control measures among Native populations. It is a complex issue.

Another core belief of the Indians also was ignored and caused catastrophic clashes in the New World. That was the Indian belief in the sacredness of traditional lands. Land belonged to everyone and was not for trading, buying, or selling. It was a belief never accepted by the newcomers, and today the Native Indian concept of land and the European idea of land ownership remain light-years apart. This issue is discussed in more detail in later chapters.

3

Medicine

Tobacco was not the only source of grief resulting from the first meetings of Amerindians and the Europeans. Within three years of Columbus setting foot on New World soil, a horrid new affliction spread through European populations. Syphilis, characterized by pustules, open ulcerations, and extreme pain, was unknown, or least unidentified, until 1495, three years after Columbus first returned from the New World.

There are conflicting theories about whether Columbus brought the primarily sexually transmitted disease to the Indians, or vice versa. King James I of England, a sourpuss who despised foreigners, tobacco, and sex with women, among many other things, said it was the Indians, through the "uncleanly ... constitution of their bodies," who gave it to the Europeans. Others believe the Europeans brought it to the Indians. Whatever the case, the first recorded syphilis epidemic in Europe occurred in 1495 and spread widely and quickly — an infliction that was terrifying and not understood.

German writer Joseph Grunpeck, who was infected about 1500, described syphilis as "a disease which is so cruel, so distressing, so appalling that until now nothing so horrifying, nothing more terrible or disgusting, has ever been known on this earth."

The spread of syphilis helped tobacco gain prominence, although little help was needed since it was spreading rapidly on its own — an amazing New World discovery. It soon would become revered as a panacea of panaceas, a plant that could cure everything.

The Indian gift plant that Columbus deemed useless and had tossed overboard became a medicine for relief from the brutal effects of syphilis. Early Spanish visitors to the Americas had seen the Indians smoke tobacco to dull pain and to use it as a salve to heal sores. Many afflicted with the new disease took up smoking tobacco to alleviate the pain.

Interest in tobacco as a medicinal plant heightened during the botanical renaissance of the mid-1500s. Not all visitors and explorers of the New World were looking for riches such as gold and silver. Newly discovered plants, and their possible medicinal uses, held much interest in Europe, and samples and information were carried back there, where the knowledge spread by word of mouth and in books. Interest in the possible medical uses of tobacco was particularly acute. Between 1537 and 1559, doctors, historians, botanists, and missionaries wrote fourteen books in eight different languages about the medicinal uses of the tobacco plant. One Jesuit author wrote that the plant was God's remedy.

Thomas Hariot, during his time in the Chesapeake region, reported that the Indian herb *uppowoc* preserved the body and opened up pores and passages and broke up any breathing obstructions: "By this means the Natives keep in excellent health, without many of the grievous diseases which often afflict us in England." Hariot "drank the smoke" as shown by the Indians, and continued to smoke after returning to England, eventually becoming addicted to tobacco.

Tobacco smoke initially was used for dulling pain and suppressing hunger. Then it was used in paste form on wounds and burns. Eventually, it became a main ingredient in enemas, ointments, syrups, and powders used for treating everything from diarrhea to colds. Tobacco was used to fight bubonic plague and cancer. Some doctors recommended it to promote better health. For centuries humans had sought a medicinal "panacea of panaceas," and in tobacco many believed they had found it.

Juan de Cárdenas, a Spanish physician in Mexico, wrote in the late 1500s: "To seek to tell the virtues and greatness of this holy herb, the ailments which can be cured by it, and have been, the evils from which it has saved thousands, would be to go on to infinity."

Despite the virtues that were ascribed to tobacco, it soon became evident that there were negative aspects to it, for, as many users soon found out, it was habit-forming. It took a grip on some individuals more than others. One reason Columbus's man Rodrigo de Jerez did prison time was because he could not renounce it before the Inquisition. Other early European users developed addictions similar to that of de Jerez, yet others were able to try it and walk away from it.

A famous example of tobacco's powerful addictive traits can be found much later with the medical history of Sigmund Freud, the Austrian neurologist and father of psychoanalysis. Freud smoked twenty cigars a day and developed an irregular heartbeat by age thirty-eight. He tried quitting but found the mental depression and other withdrawal symptoms too much to bear. He wrote: "Soon after giving up smoking there were tolerable days. Then there came suddenly a severe affection of the heart, worse than I ever had when smoking.... And with it an oppression of mood in which images of dying and farewell scenes replaced the more usual fantasies.... The organic disturbances have lessened in the last couple of days; the hypo-manic mood continues.... It is annoying for a doctor who has to be concerned all day long with neurosis not to know whether he is suffering from a justifiable or a hypochondriacal depression."

Freud developed cancer of the mouth and jaw and underwent numerous surgeries. He tried more than once to stop smoking but could not tolerate life without tobacco. He died of cancer at age eighty-three, still a smoker of cigars.

Today, despite cessation programs and chemical aids, some people still find it difficult to quit, even those who, like Freud, develop cancer. Researchers connected to Harvard Medical School in Boston reported early in 2012 that after studying more than five thousand cancer patients they learned that 14 percent of those who smoked at the time of lung cancer diagnosis were still smoking five months later.

The University of Waterloo found in a 2011 study that nearly one-half of smokers surveyed had tried to quit in the previous year. Six in ten smokers who tried to quit used some form of cessation aid while 47 percent used stop-smoking medications, including nicotine-replacement therapy.

The fact that tobacco is addictive was realized early on; however, what made the plant addictive remained unknown. Experimentation later found that tobacco contained something that set it apart from other plants, a poisonous alkaloid that came to be called *nicotine.*

Nicotine is the name created to honour Jean Nicot de Villemain (1530–1600), the French ambassador to Portugal from 1559 to 1561. Nicot had been sent to Portugal to try to negotiate the future marriage of a six-year-old French princess to the five-year-old King Sebastian of Portugal. He failed, but returned to France with tobacco plants and introduced snuff (a form of pulverized tobacco inhaled through the nose that had been used by some Indians in the Americas) to the French court. He gave Queen Catherine Medici snuff to help treat the migraine headaches suffered by her son, François II. Once introduced to the French court, it became popular among the European elite. The French took to calling tobacco the "*herbe a tous les maux,*" the plant against pain and evil, and, later, since Nicot was the first to tell the people of France about the healing powers of tobacco, the plant became known as *nicotiane.*

Nicot experimented with medicinal uses for the plant and distributed news of his work, which was detailed and well recorded, even though he was not a physician. In one experiment he reported using tobacco to heal a cancerous growth on a boy's cheek. So great was the hype about the curative properties of tobacco that English school children were forced to smoke daily to protect themselves from the great bubonic plague of 1665–66.

Three centuries passed before nicotine in tobacco was identified as a poison. Two Germans, Dr. Wilhelm Heinrich Posselt and chemist Karl Ludwig Reimann, isolated nicotine in 1828, more than three hundred years after tobacco's introduction to Europeans. That knowledge cooled enthusiasm for the plant, and medicinal uses began to fade. Until then, however, there had been few warning voices, and these were smothered by the awe and clamouring over reported cures of every type of affliction.

Today there is renewed interest in nicotine as a drug for controlling the symptoms of Tourette's syndrome and other neurological disorders such as schizophrenia and Alzheimer's disease. Scientists have noted a high prevalence of smoking among schizophrenics, and that smoking gives them short term normalization of some effects of the disease. Also, studies indicate that nicotine delivered intravenously to non-smoking Alzheimer's patients can improve long-term recall and attention span, although increases in symptoms of anxiety and depression are also seen.

Poisons such as nicotine often can be taken in tiny doses to improve health. Warfarin is an example. Used as a rat poison originally, Warfarin is taken by hundreds of thousands of humans around the world to thin blood to prevent strokes and to improve heart functions.

Lab experiments are being conducted in Toronto to determine if tobacco plants can be genetically engineered to help produce cheaper cancer drugs.

<—>

As the popularity of tobacco increased, demand and trade rose in step. The flow of tobacco from the New World after Columbus started as a trickle, then became a surge, then a flood. Sailors returning from the newly discovered lands carried back smoking materials and techniques, and the smoking habit was quickly picked up by many more people with the connections and the money to get tobacco. Other New World travellers, seeing potential medicinal benefits, brought back seeds, plants, and cultivating techniques.

Spain was at the forefront of this trade because of its New World discoveries, and its quickness in starting colonization. It kept a firm hold on tobacco and its other botanical discoveries because of a shrewd move by Philip II of Spain, who in 1570 ordered assessment of all medicinal herbs, plants, trees, and seeds in Mexico. His interest was not solely scientific: Spain was getting many of its medicines from the Far East and this involved paying the expenses of traders and various other middlemen. It made economic sense to learn more about medicinal plants from the new colonies.

Spain's discovery and colonization of the New World lifted it to the pinnacle of its power and influence. Its bases in the Caribbean were stepping stones to the conquests of Mexico and parts of South America where Amerindian cultures were replaced by plantation colonies. The riches that flowed from its new colonies helped to create a golden age for literature, music, and art in Spain.

Spanish influence was everywhere. Philip II even became co-ruler of England after marrying Queen Mary I. She died four years after the marriage, and, worried about losing his influence in England, Philip pursued the new queen, Elizabeth I, who coyly held him off.

The Spanish were decades ahead of the English, French, and Dutch in exploring and settling the New World. It took those other three nations until the 1620s and 1630s to begin establishing colonies in the Caribbean. England had tried establishing tobacco plantations around the Amazon delta and the coast of Guyana, but they were pushed out by Spanish troops.

The Spanish grip on the southern regions of the New World forced the English to attempt colonies far up the North American East Coast, where the weather was much more hostile. It was the same for the Dutch, who finally had to settle on Manhattan as a place to set down New World roots. As for the French, they were still exploring the St. Lawrence River looking for gold more than one hundred years after Columbus.

They all craved the riches of the New World, but without colonies of their own, they were reduced to plundering Spanish ships returning home. From them they stole not only bullion and other riches, but tobacco, which was in short supply to meet Europe's medicinal demands, and the growing appetite for tobacco for pleasure.

4

Stealing to Inhale

Tobacco was incidental booty for the sea dogs who preyed on Spanish ships returning from the Americas. They were after the silver and gold aboard the treasure-laden ships they attacked, but when they found tobacco, they gladly took it. Medical demand for the plant flourished, while recreational uses such as smoking, chewing, and snuffing increased as more people tried, liked, and became addicted to tobacco. Buccaneers could sell it easily because tobacco demand was growing faster than production in the New World.

Tobacco's popularity in England was boosted in the late 1500s by an unexpected source. Queen Elizabeth I, known as the Virgin Queen, helped popularize tobacco when one of her favourite knights, Sir Walter Raleigh, introduced her to smoking. Raleigh had travelled to America where he learned about smoking; after his return, he offered a demonstration to the English court. The queen, a lively and adventurous woman, took some puffs from a pipe offered by Raleigh and became so queasy that some courtiers thought Raleigh had poisoned her. She recovered quickly, however, and, impressed by the effects of tobacco, had the countess of Nottingham and her maids try a pipeful. Smoking then became a craze among courtiers, who practised smoking tricks such as the "Gulpe" and "Retention." Such high-level acceptance helped spread the habit throughout the kingdom. Besides being a popular medicinal product, tobacco in England now became a pleasure craze.

In the 1960s, American comedian Bob Newhart had a hilarious monologue on Raleigh bringing tobacco to England. It probably did more to popularize that little piece of history than any history book.

Without colonies to grow tobacco, the English and others encouraged sea kings like Sir Francis Drake, John Hawkins, Henry Morgan, and Daniel Montbars, who terrorized Spanish shipping lanes and colonies, stealing huge amounts of tobacco, among other valuable commodities. Some were privateers, government-sanctioned pirates paid to plunder by nations trying to compete with Spain. Others were independent pirates, who worked for themselves and kept the booty for themselves.

The English legalized privateers, also called buccaneers, as a low-cost, unofficial way of warring against Spain. The British Crown gave the nod to piracy, then looked the other way, in exchange for a share of the booty.

The Spanish tried protecting their treasure ships by travelling in convoys. This helped to lessen their losses, and even when a ship or two was taken, the loss was of little concern. No matter what the buccaneers managed to steal, there always was more in the flourishing colonies. The Spanish continued to thrive, driven by silver, gold, sugar, spices, and the obsession with spreading Catholicism throughout the world.

Spanish success chafed the English, and the French, who had tried to establish colonies but had failed miserably. The failures were discouraging because after decades of watching the Spanish and Portuguese advance in the New World, the English and French desperately wanted North American colonies that would build industries, create new wealth, and expand their power and influence against Spain.

The English and French attempted to establish themselves between the late 1500s and early 1600s, but many of their settlers starved, froze, or were hatcheted to death by hostile Indians.

In 1584 Elizabeth I became intrigued by a plan spun out by her friend Walter Raleigh, a sometime explorer-adventurer, businessman, and indefatigable promoter. The queen granted Raleigh patents for discovery and colonization in America. He dispatched ships carrying about one hundred male settlers across the Atlantic. They eventually settled on Roanoke Island in the Chesapeake Bay area. They found life miserable there, however, and after a while abandoned the place and returned to England, unaware that a relief ship had been dispatched to find them. The relief ship found them gone, and, following instructions, left fifteen men behind to retain a British foothold on the area. Indians attacked the little settlement, and so the men took to the ocean in small boats. They were never seen again.

In 1587 a second group of one hundred men, accompanied this time by seventeen women, and some children, landed at Roanoke. The little settlement that had been established was a charred ruin, but they set to work rebuilding it. They struggled along, unaided by any help from Britain because war with Spain prevented relief ships from returning to the area until 1591. When a ship finally arrived, the settlement was deserted. The only clue to what had happened to the settlers was the word *Croatoan*, which had been carved into a tree. The Croatoans were friendly Indians who lived south of the settlement.

Scholars have tried to piece together the fate of the settlers. Some speculate they had a tough time surviving alone and so joined a tribe of friendly Indians. Others say hostile Indians killed them all. Still others speculate that the settlers were killed by Spanish troops who might have travelled up from Florida, fulfilling Spain's desire to stop the English from ever settling in the New World.

The French did not fare much better in their settlement efforts. In 1541 Jacques Cartier, the "discoverer of Canada," was ordered to return to the New World and establish a French colony. He landed his party of convicts at the site of present-day Quebec City. They established a settlement that they named Charlesbourg-Royal, where they tried raising cattle and growing kitchen vegetables. They abandoned it in 1543 after disease, foul weather, and hostile Indians drove the would-be settlers to despair.

That ended the French plans for Canada, until 1599, when a sixteen-person trading post was established at Tadoussac, where the Saguenay and St. Lawrence Rivers meet. Only a few of the men survived the first winter there.

French colonization attempts finally took root in the early 1600s, when Samuel de Champlain moved a struggling settlement on the St. Croix River across the Bay of Fundy to Port Royal in present-day Nova Scotia. Following that, he went on to establish a new colony, what would eventually become Quebec City, in 1608.

At roughly the same time — 1606 — King James I, who ascended the English throne after Elizabeth, chartered two joint stock companies: the Virginia Company of London and the Virginia Company of Plymouth. They were to establish colonies in what we now know as the State of Virginia. Their purpose was to create wealth for England from the resources of the New World. The Plymouth Company established a colony along Maine's Kennebec River, but it failed after a year. The London Company built Jamestown on the James River, a major river draining into Chesapeake Bay.

The London Company wanted its settlers to build industries that would create profit from sassafras, lumber, pitch and tar, glass making, and soap ashes. That colony teetered on the edge of failure until a second wave of settlers was sent out to strengthen it.

The five hundred colonists of the second wave sailed from England in 1609, but were caught in a hurricane. One of the nine ships, the *Sea Venture*, was leaking badly and was grounded in Bermuda where the 150 crew and settlers onboard used parts from the ship to build two smaller ships that set sail and finally arrived at the Jamestown colony a year later.

The new arrivals found that 80 percent of the six hundred colonists there had starved to death, died of disease, or been killed in confrontations with the Indians. The future did not look promising. The new arrivals set to work, however, and some took an interest in learning more about the planting and cultivation of Indian crops — including tobacco.

Interest in and demand for tobacco was increasing in England, but supplies were limited, and therefore prices were exorbitant. For instance, one pound of tobacco in the very early 1600s cost hundreds of times more than a tankard of beer. The price of a pound of tobacco could buy a man a prostitute for every night of the week, and beer for as many friends as he might gather in a couple of large public houses.

Some colonists could see that raising tobacco for export and sale could produce revenue that would help the colony survive and grow. The key was to improve Indian tobacco to make it more acceptable to the growing smoking public.

The same idea had occurred to some in Europe too. There, cultivation experiments were already under way with plants and seeds brought back from the Americas. Raleigh himself grew Indian tobacco from seeds brought from the deserted Roanoke colony, and experimented with improving it. He constantly promoted this homegrown tobacco as his preferred smoke, but the rapidly expanding smoking public disagreed. The smoking public in England found the Indian wild tobacco from the North American East Coast strong and bitter and of poor quality. English consumers preferred the milder, pleasanter tobacco from the southern Spanish colonies. Spanish tobacco was the best, but with supplies tightly controlled, English access to a good smoke was mainly through piracy.

If the English colonists could grow tobacco as good as the Spanish product, their foothold in America would be firmly established.

5

Saviour of Virginia

One of the early settlers in Jamestown was John Rolfe. He settled into colonial life alone, despondent, and looking for something to keep his mind off the tragic events he'd suffered since leaving England. He and his wife were aboard the leaky *Sea Venture* when it was run aground deliberately at Bermuda to prevent it from sinking. While they were on the island, Rolfe's wife gave birth to a daughter, who they named Bermuda, but the baby died soon after birth.

It had taken ten months before the crew and colonists had been able to build two new ships from the salvage of the *Sea Venture* and other materials scrounged from the island. They named the ships *Patience* and *Deliverance*, and sailed north. When they did reach Jamestown, however, Rolfe's wife died, and he faced the challenge of starting a new life alone in the bush colony.

He took interest in the coarse Indian tobacco that grew wild in Virginia, and experimented with it. He sought to improve it, to breed it so that it more closely resembled the tobacco grown by the Spanish and Portuguese, which was preferred because it was milder to smoke. He experimented with growing and curing methods, and while doing so became a dedicated smoker.

His best results came from tobacco seeds that likely were smuggled from the Spanish West Indies colonies. The Spanish controlled the West Indian tobacco trade, trying to ensure that the English never received any advantage that might help them become established in America. The Spanish monarchy had placed restrictions on tobacco growing and exports in 1606, and exportation of seeds was punishable by death.

It is not recorded where or how Rolfe got his seeds, but probably they were contraband. He crossbred his tobaccos, and his experiments produced a milder, sweeter tobacco. After two years of experimentation, he had produced a fragrant new strain that he shipped to England in 1613. The new Virginians, led by Rolfe and his tobacco experiments, had found a product that promised to give England's American colony the basis for an economy, albeit a precarious one.

Ralph Hamor, then-secretary of Virginia, wrote that Rolfe helped the colony with his experiments and by sharing them with others. "I may not forget the gentleman worthie of much commendations, which first tooke the pains to make triall thereof, his name Mr. John Rolfe, Anno Domini 1612, partly for the love he hath a long time borne unto it, and partly to raise commodity to the adventurers," wrote Hamor.

Life in Virginia remained precarious, however, because of the isolation and Indian threats. While Rolfe was shipping his first crop of new tobacco to England, there were Indian troubles, which resulted in the colonists kidnapping Pocahontas, the daughter of Chief Powhatan, a local Indian chief, and using her as a bargaining chip. They brought her to Jamestown in hopes of exchanging her for English prisoners and weapons held by Powhatan. There was no exchange, however, and Pocahontas settled into colonial life and learned English.

Rolfe fell in love with her, but was tortured by the idea of possibly marrying an Indian. He sought advice, prayed, and finally accepted that her conversion to Christianity made it possible for them to marry. Their marriage, sanctioned by Powhatan, brought some years of relative peace between the colonists and the Indians.

The marriage, peace with the Indians, more experimentation, and knowledge likely gained from Pocahontas, helped Rolfe continually improve his tobacco crop and his methods, and success spread through the colony.

His work was not fully appreciated back home in England. The English government wanted its American colonists to thrive, but it wanted them to do so by producing useful stuff such as food and ship-building materials. King James leaned hard on colony governors and Virginia administrators to discourage and restrict tobacco growing and trade. These disincentives, which included bounties for growing non-tobacco crops, did not stop Rolfe and others from developing a tobacco industry.

For the Virginians, a tobacco crop was worth six times more than corn. As tobacco use spread, demand increased, and the Virginians were determined to improve their tobacco and meet the burgeoning demand. Rolfe and his fellow colonists continued to pursue improvements. For instance they used the Indian technique of topping tobacco plants as they started to flower. This directed more of the plant's energy into the leaves, producing a thicker, more vital leaf that ripened earlier.

Rolfe's Virginia tobacco began the tobacco revolution. Virginia tobacco, mild and sweeter and easier to inhale than the original, native tobacco, eventually dominated the tobacco industry. In 1616 Virginia shipped a ton and half of tobacco to England. The next year it shipped 18,800 pounds. Between 1625 and 1631, average yearly shipments were 362,000 pounds. By 1700 that figure was thirty-eight million pounds. By the time of the American Revolution, Virginia was the wealthiest of the Thirteen Colonies.

Tobacco's commercial ascendancy was dramatic, and it began to dominate colonial life. Tobacco was used as money in Virginia.

When, in 1621, a cargo of twelve young women made its way to the colony, each one was valued at 120 pounds of the best leaf.

In 1696 state law required that Virginia's ministers be paid with sixteen thousand pounds of tobacco annually. The law provided that "a competent and sufficient provision for the clergy will be the only means to supply this dominion with able and faithful Ministers whereby the glory of God may be advanced, the church propagated, and the people edified."

Commercial tobacco growing spread through what became known as New England. Maryland was settled in 1634 and settlers made it their principal crop. It was also grown in areas of what became New York City, originally a Dutch colony that took in some English who had religious differences with colonists who had settled the Boston area.

In Virginia a man's wealth was measured in pounds of tobacco. Fines could be paid with tobacco. Tobacco was life, and it had assured the survival of the English in America.

6

Le tabac canadien

The French also learned about tobacco from the Indians, but, unlike the English, did nothing to develop it as an economic driver. They had found something they thought better: the fur trade. Tobacco, for the early French in Canada, was something to grow for personal use, not for extensive trade.

While the English had problems keeping the Virginians focused on growing non-tobacco crops, the French problem was trying to get young settlers to stay home and grow anything. The men yearned for the western horizons, where life was wild and free, and riches were to be found in furs. Those who did stay at home followed the agriculture practices of the Indians. They grew vegetables, hemp, and some tobacco, which was of the Indian variety — bitingly strong and not well flavoured.

The Indians themselves mixed their tobacco with ground leaves and bark from other plants. Some tribes called their smoking mixture *kinnikinnick*, which in the Algonquian tongue means "that which is mixed." Kinnikinnick was milder than pure tobacco and was smoked in a pipe. It soon became a favourite of the French settlers and coureurs du bois, the French colonial adventurers.

Early Quebec farmers, habitants, grew small amounts of rough Indian-style tobacco and cured it in the open air. Many chopped their tobacco daily, and the process produced a unique, homegrown tobacco that became known as *le tabac canadien*. Some might have preferred the milder and sweeter Brazilian or Caribbean tobaccos, but it was hard to get and expensive. It was simpler to smoke homegrown tobacco, and the Quebec settlers got so used to it that tabac canadien became not only a tradition but a statement of distinct French-Canadian culture.

Explorers and fur traders carried their tobacco pouches and pipes across the country's waterways and portages, smoking to relax, to suppress their hunger, or for simple enjoyment. They were supplied by those who stayed behind on the farms, growing tobacco chiefly for personal use, while the New Englanders began growing for the world.

There were no incentives for habitants to grow tobacco for sale. The French government had early on prohibited the retail sale of tobacco in New France. One reason was that the French government wanted to protect the developing interests of its tropical colonies, where it believed tobacco was easier to cultivate. Tobacco growing in Quebec was not encouraged by the French government until 1735, and then commercial varieties such as Petit Canadien and Rose Quesnel were grown. Although there was then some tobacco cultivation as a commercial enterprise, the fur trade remained *the* industry of New France. In 1735 furs accounted for 70 percent of the colony's exports, although the colony continued to struggle.

At the same time, the British American colonies to the south blossomed on tobacco profits, and boasted two million inhabitants by 1735. The British strength in North America continued to outpace that of New France until 1763, when the Seven Years' War between the two nations ended with New France being ceded to Britain.

Tobacco growing in Quebec continued under British rule, but again it was grown mainly for home use until late in the 1800s, when new curing techniques and automation allowed for the mass production of cigarettes and pushed Canada ahead as a major tobacco producer.

A founder of the Quebec tobacco industry was Bartholomé Houde, who opened a tobacco shop in Quebec City in 1841 selling pipe and chewing tobacco and snuff. He specialized in pipe tobacco made with tabac canadien grown in the Joliette region. He employed a clerk named François-Xavier Dussault, who later became his partner and his son-in-law after marrying Houde's daughter Adelaide in 1869.

Houde retired in 1882. Dussault took over the business, enlarging it and buying more modern equipment. He organized a troupe of travelling salesmen, who spread Houde and Co. tobacco products from Halifax to Vancouver. The business prospered and the couple soon became one of the wealthiest in the city.

François-Xavier and Adelaide built one of the most famous grand houses in Quebec City, the Château du Faubourg. It was designed by architect Joseph Ferdinand Peachy in the 1880s as a classic example of French Second Empire architecture. Today it has been restored and is operated as a private bed and breakfast.

François-Xavier died in 1891, and Adelaide took over the business with the help of her two sons. She became known in Quebec City as "*la Régente*" and was believed to be one of the wealthiest women in Canada at the time. The Dussault sons operated the business when she died in 1895, but began facing increasing competition, both locally and from American Tobacco Ltd., which was trying to dominate the Canadian market. There is one story that American firm gave out free tobacco on the streets of Quebec as part of its plan to take over the Canadian market.

American offered to buy Houde, but the boys resisted. American increased the pressure, and the Dussault boys gave in and sold in 1903, staying on in executive positions. The Houde name remained until 1943; eventually, American Tobacco was absorbed by Imperial Tobacco, which still operates out of Quebec today.

In Upper Canada, which became Ontario, Indians had grown tobacco long before the arrival of the Europeans. The French discovered an Iroquoian-speaking people growing tobacco along the shores of Georgian Bay, in what is now the Collingwood region. They called them *gens du petún* or "tobacco Indians," because they were skilled at tobacco cultivation. Some researchers believe that the Petuns grew large fields of tobacco for trade with other tribes.

Ontario tobacco growing gained prominence after the American Revolution, when United Empire Loyalists streamed into Canada in 1783–84. Some settled along the north shore of Lake Erie, bringing with them tobacco seeds and expertise at growing gained in the U.S. tobacco-growing regions.

Commercial production tobacco began in Ontario around 1800, and by 1840 long tobacco-curing barns dotted the landscapes in Essex and Kent counties. Flue curing — a process in which hot air is passed through pipes (flues) from exterior fires into the curing barns — came to Canada in 1900. This process turned dark air-cured tobacco into bright golden leaf better suited for cigarettes.

The growth of the Ontario tobacco industry is best illustrated by the story of George Elias Tuckett, who founded the Tuckett Tobacco Company of Hamilton in 1857. Tuckett established a small business rolling cigars, then opened a cigar store in London. His wife sold his cigars at markets and fairs in and around Hamilton. Five years after starting the cigar business, he gave that up and began to make plug chewing tobacco for which there was a great demand.

While Southwestern Ontario was growing increasing amounts of tobacco, much of the raw leaf needed for smoking and chewing came from the United States. The U.S. Civil War interrupted that flow, and there is a story that Tuckett and a partner went behind Confederate lines to get Virginia tobacco for their business. The

Photo: Ron Poling

Commercial production tobacco began in Ontario around 1800, and by 1840 tobacco-curing barns dotted the landscapes in Essex and Kent counties. Flue curing came to Canada in 1900 and involved passing hot air through pipes (flues) from exterior fires into curing barns. This process turned dark air-cured tobacco into bright golden leaf better suited for cigarettes.

business prospered, producing plug tobacco, cigars, and eventually cigarettes. It grew from seventy employees in 1868 to four hundred in the 1880s. The company was bought by Imperial Tobacco in 1930.

Imperial remains the largest tobacco company in Canada. It was incorporated in 1908, having acquired the Montreal tobacco companies D. Ritchie & Co. and the American Cigarette Co. The second-largest is Rothmans, Benson & Hedges Incorporated, which began as the Rock City Tobacco Company, started in 1899 as a Houde competitor.

The third major Canadian tobacco manufacturer is JTI-Macdonald Corporation, a company that also began in Quebec, and like the rest has gone through a series of buyouts by international companies. RJ Reynolds International bought it in 1974, then sold it to Japan Tobacco in 1999.

Macdonald, famous for its Scottish lass on packs of Export 'A', was started in 1858 by two Scottish brothers. William C.

Source: Delhi Tobacco Museum & Heritage Centre — Photo Collection

The tobacco industry was a huge employer in North America before the 1964 U.S. Surgeon General's Report on the dangers of smoking. For instance, the Imperial Tobacco plant in Aylmer, Ontario, employed up to six hundred full-time and seasonal workers until it closed in 2007. Many people, like these men, originally were employed to stand at tables sorting leaves and tying them in bundles for hanging in kilns.

Macdonald later became the sole owner. He was an odd man, who made a fortune from plug tobacco, but hated cigarettes and refused to make them. The company did not make cigarettes until after his death in 1917. He was a frugal, lifetime bachelor and willed the business to the two sons of his company manager, David Stewart.

Macdonald had only one major cigarette brand, but Export 'A' had extremely loyal followers because of the Second World War. Wartime shortages resulted in inferior cigarettes sometimes, but Macdonald was adamant that soldiers get the best quality cigarettes ahead of civilians. Many returning soldiers never forgot that and were forever loyal to the green Export 'A' packages with the Scottish lassie.

<—>

Quebec's obsession with the fur trade resulted in its tobacco industry lagging far behind that of Virginia. Despite its slow start, however, the Canadian tobacco industry took flight around the start of the twentieth century. Canadian cigarette consumption rose from 89 million cigarettes in 1898, to 184 million in 1903, and to 277 million in 1906.

Quebec and Ontario remain the centres of Canadian tobacco growing and cigarette manufacturing today. The major tobacco companies, founded by Houde, Tuckett, and Macdonald, remain a presence there and have been joined by major Native tobacco companies, such as Rainbow Tobacco and Grand River Enterprises.

Tobacco is graded before sale, and grading was once done by taking samples of leaves with a manual punch.

Source: Delhi Tobacco Museum & Heritage Centre — Photo Collection

7

Magnificent Contradiction

With the European discovery of Indian tobacco came the great contradiction that governments continue to struggle with today. Early governments, often driven by religious influences, saw tobacco as evil and tried to stop its use by means of coercion, restrictions, and taxation policies that made it financially more difficult for common people to obtain it. Five hundred years later, governments are still wrestling with the evils of smoking, while pocketing the fortunes that it produces.

For more than five hundred years, tobacco has been the world's magnificent contradiction. It soothes, yet sickens. Early political and religious leaders mostly despised it, while their subjects fell in love with it. To stop tobacco use, governments taxed it, then became addicted to the revenue they derived from taxing it.

The introduction to Europe of smoking in the early 1500s must have been shocking. Imagine someone in a tavern or on a street corner sucking on a burning reed, then expelling the smoke through his mouth and nose. It had to be the work of the Devil and his witches! But once a person drank in the smoke, its nicotine could make one feel like it was the work of the angels.

Fire and smoke were associated with Satan, yet the early Spanish priests trying to understand Indian beliefs fell under tobacco's spell. They took to this product of Satan first by snuffing it, then smoking it. The reasoning behind the priestly use of the weed was totally contradictory. Benedetto Stella, a priest who wrote a treatise on tobacco in 1669, said it reduced sexual urges. "I say that the use of tobacco taken moderately is not only useful but even necessary for the priests, monks, friars, and other religious [men] who desire to lead a chaste life and repress those sensual urges that sometimes assail them. The natural cause of lust is heat and humidity. When it is dried out through the use of tobacco, these libidinous surges are not felt so powerfully."

Others held the view that tobacco increased sexual desire. Centuries later, of course, smoking became sexy, especially in the movies.

One of the clearest contradictions regarding the use of tobacco was seen in the Catholic Church's early history in Spanish America. Indians insisted on smoking in church, so in 1575 the Church issued an order that forbid smoking inside churches. This was not enough, however; so many priests had become addicted to tobacco that the Church had to order that no priest could chew, smoke, or snuff tobacco before celebrating mass.

Despite Stella's views on the benefits of tobacco use, for many religious and political leaders of those times, there was nothing good about tobacco. Campaigns against tobacco use started early and were filled with histrionics. Early prohibitions against tobacco use in some cultures were severe. Murad the Cruel, Sultan of the Ottoman Empire, sometimes roamed about looking to catch people smoking in defiance of his ban. He caught thousands, who he beheaded, dismembered, or somehow made suffer before they died.

Bans existed early in the Far East. Japan imprisoned smokers and confiscated their worldly goods. China outlawed the use and growing of tobacco in 1638 and made offences punishable by decapitation. In India, Persia, and Turkey, the death penalty also was prescribed as a cure for the habit.

The first smoking ban on record was enacted by Pope Urban VII in 1590. He ordered that anyone who chewed, smoked, or snuffed tobacco in the porch of a church, or inside the church itself, would risk excommunication. That was expanded by Pope Urban VIII, who forbade Catholics from snuffing tobacco, because it caused sneezing, which he considered very close to "sexual ecstasy." The ban on tobacco use around churches was repealed by Pope Benedict XIII, an avid smoker.

In 1627 Russian courts introduced a tobacco ban during which tobacco users were penalized by having their lips slit or noses cut off. At one point any Russian caught with tobacco was tortured until he gave the name of his supplier. Czar Peter the Great (1682–1725) lifted the bans when he realized that his treasury could be fattened by tobacco. During a famous tour of Europe, he signed a deal giving English merchants a monopoly licence on tobacco imports to Russia. Foreign growers were then invited to start plantations in what is now Ukraine. The tobacco grown there was of such good quality that it produced the world-renowned Davidoff cigars.

In 1635 Louis XIII of France restricted tobacco sales to apothecaries, where it could be bought by prescription only. A snuff user himself, the king decided to repeal the law two years later.

King James I of England didn't cut off smokers' heads, but certainly vented his spleen on the topic of smoking by his subjects, thousands of whom were joining the smoking ranks, which swelled by the day. His predecessor, Elizabeth I, had found smoking amusing, but James, her Scottish cousin, who took the throne because Elizabeth left no heir, considered it a disgusting practice that needed to be banished from English life.

He had accepted the medicinal use of tobacco as "a physick to preserve health," but thought it was being taken excessively by "a number of riotous and disordered persons of mean and base conditions." So, in 1604 he wrote and distributed his famous *Counterblaste to Tobacco*, a polemic that was one of the earliest anti-smoking publications. *Counterblaste* argued that just because an inferior race discovered something, there was no reason for a superior race to debase itself by using it:

> … what honour or policie can moove us to imitate the barbarous and beastly maners of the wilde, god-lesse, and slauish Indians, especially in so vile and stinking a custome? Have you not reason then to bee ashamed, and to forbeare this filthie noveltie, so basely grounded, so foolishly received, and so grossely mistaken in the right use thereof? In your abuse thereof, sinning against God, harming yourselves both in persons and goods, and taking also thereby the markes and notes of vanitie upon you: by the custome thereof, making your selves to be wondered at by all forraine civil Nations, and by all strangers that come among you, to be scorned and contemned. A custome lothsome to the eye, hatefull to the Nose, harmefull to the braine, dangerous to the Lungs, and in the blacke stinking fume thereof, neerest resembling the horrible Stigian smoke of the pit that is bottomelesse.

Counterblaste was the rant of a frustrated king who knew he was fighting a losing battle. It was largely ignored, sometimes even ridiculed. Despite this, James issued various other proclamations against tobacco, including one from his deathbed in 1624 that prohibited domestic tobacco production.

His campaigns against tobacco had little effect. His tobacco proclamations were ignored, much as his *Counterblaste* was. His failures should have been a lesson to anti-tobacco campaigners of the future. Yelling and pointing fingers, even slitting lips, does little to stop people from smoking. Understanding, education, and medical help, when needed, are the proven best tools for reducing tobacco use.

King James's efforts against tobacco did much to help create the magnificent contradiction, however. When he ascended the throne, there was only a nominal duty on tobacco. He immediately raised this import tax by an incredible 4,000 percent, in hopes of ridding his kingdom of the vile product. All the king's ranting, and all the king's fiscal burdens on tobacco, could not stop the spreading yearn of the people. It did, however, promote smuggling, which he had to legislate against later when contraband became a significant problem.

The Spanish Crown put restrictions on tobacco a couple of years after King James began his anti-tobacco work. That was not so much to prevent people from smoking it as it was to stop other countries from obtaining the milder and sweeter tobacco found in the Spanish colonies. Spain ordered that the sale of tobacco or seed to foreigners be punishable by death. That didn't stop others from getting it through theft, diversion, and smuggling, however, and so it ended up in the hands of buyers elsewhere — buyers such as the experimental grower from Virginia, John Rolfe.

The Spanish government then dove headlong into the tobacco business. It grabbed control of all tobacco, and in 1636 established Tabacalera, the world's first tobacco company. It also opened tobacco shops in Spain and ordered all tobacco sold in those places subject to another tax.

France discouraged tobacco production in Quebec. One reason was that habitants growing and exporting tobacco there would have been competition for its southern colonies. The powerfully manipulative Cardinal Richelieu, the king's first minister, had high ambitions for French colonial power in the Caribbean, and in 1635 formed the Compagnie des Îsles d'Amériques, which encouraged French colonists to go to the Caribbean to grow tobacco.

Besides not wanting Quebec to compete with its Caribbean colonies in the tobacco trade, France did not wish to encourage anything that might affect the coin for the realm that French Canada was producing without tobacco. The fur trade was lucrative, with the additional spinoffs of exploration and discovery of new North American territories. There was little incentive for the colony to grow tobacco, apart from for domestic consumption, and, in fact, the first tobacco exports from Canada to France did not occur until 1739.

There were prohibitions against tobacco use in New France as well. Citizens were forbidden from smoking. They were not even allowed to carry tobacco on the streets for almost one hundred years, until the British conquest. Retail sale of tobacco was forbidden for a while as well, which strengthened the tradition of growing your own at home.

Even in early New England, religious views toward the plant brought prohibitions in some areas. In 1629 Massachusetts settlers were forbidden from planting any tobacco, which already was doing well in Virginia, except for small amounts that could be used as medicine.

The stiff moral opposition began to bend, however, as more people persuaded themselves, and others, that this deviant behaviour was not so evil. Business and government saw that trans-Atlantic trade in tobacco was good for the economy. Smoke from the plant was soothing, and its addictive properties increasingly made it a friend of many. As more people used it, fewer saw it as deviant behaviour.

Those who did see smoking as a problem were often firm and outspoken. Four hundred years after the introduction of tobacco to Europeans, car maker Henry Ford became a powerful voice against tobacco. Smoking had become common and popular when Ford published *The Case Against the Little White Slaver*, the 1914 pamphlet that contained many testimonials against smoking. One of the testimonials was from Thomas Edison, who wrote: "The injurious agent in cigarettes comes principally from the burning paper wrapper. The substance thereby formed is called *acrolein*. It has a violent action on the nerve centers, producing degeneration of the cells of the brain, which is quite rapid among boys. Unlike most narcotics, this degeneration is permanent and uncontrollable. I employ no person who smokes cigarettes."

The Ford Motor Company prohibited smoking in its assembly plants and its dealerships. Even buyers at Ford dealerships were forbidden from smoking while shopping for a car. The company did not allow smoking on company premises until 1947, long after Ford had died.

By the end of the seventeenth century, tobacco use had been vindicated by social pressures, transformed in the European mind from the frightening work of the Devil to a legitimate pleasure that made money for rulers and their governments. Whether it was taxed to prohibit use or just to raise money, it was taxed more and more, resulting in a situation today where in many jurisdictions taxes form the largest portion of the price of tobacco.

Whenever the gap between tax-inflated price and actual market value has widened, however, the appeal to smugglers and counterfeiters becomes irresistible. Anyone trying to make money by exploiting the price gap created between legally obtained, highly taxed cigarettes and cheaper, smuggled ones has found little objection from tobacco users. Tobacco smugglers offer savings at the expense of governments, which many people consider great squanderers of hard-earned money. It is a strange form of social vindication, in which smugglers are considered the lesser of two evils because they save common folks money that spendthrift governments try to take from them.

In the early days of the adoption of tobacco by settlers and by Europeans, it was social vindication that vaulted tobacco into its critical economic and social role in world affairs. Although much of the seventeenth-century world saw tobacco as a deviant drug, its use to be condemned and persecuted out of existence, economic interests, supported by powerful groups with much to gain, championed tobacco use, making it a highly prized substance, until it became the symbol of glamour seen in 1940s movies. Tobacco also became cool because it made a lot of people a lot of money. Governments in particular.

8

The Cigarette

The kings, queens, and other important folks who ran governments in the 1600s did not realize it, but when they introduced the taxation of tobacco, they were only skimming the surface of the pot. The pot was wider and much deeper than they ever could have imagined.

Wide-scale daily use of tobacco did not occur until more than two hundred years after the first Europeans observed it among the Amerindians. Lack of supply prevented regular use. Although tobacco was wanted, indeed craved, it took time to put it into usable form. It had to be grown, cured, chopped, fashioned into a product, packaged, and distributed.

Pulverizing tobacco leaves into snuff, rolling it into cigars, or compressing it into chewing blocks was done with hand tools and was labour-intensive. No means had been found to shorten the process of getting tobacco from the fields and to consumers.

The time-consuming process of producing and processing it, plus government prohibitions and taxation, limited tobacco's availability. While growing numbers of people loved tobacco, much of the world still did not understand it and so opposed it. The opposition to tobacco could not compete, however, against the power of the addiction. Also, the curative potential of the plant, mostly misguided, and the clinking of coins falling into treasuries, helped the weed along a path to social acceptance.

Tobacco's main attraction is its ability to deliver nicotine to the body. While many early users were happy to smoke it in pipes, or snuff it, or even chew it, widespread acceptance of tobacco required an efficient and inexpensive means of delivery. Different cultures have had different ways of administering nicotine to themselves, but most were awkward, costly, or both. Those who preferred to chew tobacco had to get it into a form that could be easily carried for whenever they wanted to bite off a piece. Those chewing tobacco also required spots to spit out the juice, a crudity that is hard to comprehend today.

Charles Dickens wrote with disgust about the chewing habit in America in 1842, and of Washington, D.C., being the headquarters of "tobacco-tinctured saliva."

> In all the public places of America, this filthy custom is recognised. In the courts of law, the judge has his spittoon, the crier his, the witness his, and the prisoner his; while the jurymen and spectators are provided for, as so many men who in the course of nature must desire to spit incessantly. In the hospitals, the students of medicine are requested, by notices upon the wall, to eject their tobacco juice into the boxes provided for that purpose, and not to discolour the stairs. In public buildings, visitors are implored, through the same agency, to squirt the essence of their quids, or "plugs," as I have heard them called by gentlemen learned in this kind of sweetmeat, into the national spittoons, and not about the bases of the marble columns. But in some parts, this custom is inseparably mixed up with every meal and morning call, and with all the transactions of social life.

Dickens also described the unsightly and unhealthy effects of chewing tobacco on the houses of Congress: "Both Houses are handsomely carpeted; but the state to which these carpets are reduced by the universal disregard of the spittoon with which every honourable member is accommodated, and the extraordinary improvements on the pattern which are squirted and dabbled upon it in every direction, do not admit of being described. I will merely observe, that I strongly recommend all strangers not to look at the floor; and if they happen to drop anything, though it be their purse, not to pick it up with an ungloved hand on any account."

Snuff was considered more elegant than chewing tobacco, but it was too expensive and too aristocratic for the masses. Cigars were neither especially elegant, nor inexpensive.

Smoking tobacco in a pipe was the least expensive and most common way of taking in tobacco smoke. There were difficulties with pipe smoking, however. For instance, the small clay pipes used by Elizabethans — known as *faerie pipes*, they were designed to use tiny amounts of expensive tobacco — broke easily and therefore could not be simply stuffed into a pocket.

Pipe smoking was also something that women found less easy to engage in as time progressed. Pipes became associated with masculinity and pipe smoking came to be considered unfeminine. French-Canadian women in rural areas smoked pipes in early times, as did women in some other parts of the world, but female pipe use declined as the 1800s progressed.

Tobacco needed a nicotine delivery system that could be mass-produced at low expense, and could be easily used by different people in different living and working conditions. A system existed in rough form among the Indians of Central and South America. As Columbus's men witnessed, many of them had their tobacco rolled in leaves, which could be set afire. They used maize, banana, and tobacco leaves, or even bark or reeds as wrappers for the tobacco.

Hernán Cortés described the great Aztec emperor Montezuma drinking a cup of cocoa and smoking tobacco in a reed after a sumptuous dinner. Various Mayan paintings show men smoking tobacco mixtures through tubes or pipes.

The Spanish picked up on the idea, using maize wrappers to wrap the tobacco, then progressing to fine papers. The smoking product created by putting tobacco inside a paper wrapper was called a *papelate*. The papelate became popular in France during the early 1800s, and the French called it the cigarette.

Early cigarettes were wrapped in whatever pieces of paper were available. Fine paper made for rolling cigarettes was available in the later 1700s, but it was expensive, and a piece for rolling each cigarette had to be torn or cut from a larger sheet.

There were various attempts at making paper especially for rolling cigarette tobacco, but there is little evidence of much commercial production until late 1796, when the Lacroix cigarette-rolling-paper company received an order from Napoleon to supply rolling papers for his troops. There are stories of Napoleon's soldiers rolling their tobacco in pages torn from books. Newspaper also was used.

Then, in 1800, a Spanish priest named Jaime Villanueva Estingo invented small dispenser packs to hold individual rolling papers. The user simply had to pull one out, put tobacco on it, and roll it into a cigarette. After the creation of this, all anyone on the move needed to smoke was a little pack of rolling paper and a pouch of minced tobacco.

Smoking was catching on, but it still was not a daily habit for many. By the mid-1800s, large numbers of people around the world were using tobacco, but irregularly and not in great amounts. Cigarettes had to be rolled by hand, or bought from people who rolled them for profit, and it has been estimated that at the time, people smoked only about forty cigarettes a year on average, fewer than one cigarette a week.

Rolling cigarettes for sale was done by artisans in the first half of the nineteenth century. A fast worker could roll one thousand or more cigarettes in a day, several a minute. The earliest rolling factories in North America were in New York City, and employed immigrants, especially Turks, who had experience with their own types of tobacco, which were becoming popular.

The biggest boost for cigarettes reputedly came as the result of a mistake by a sleepy teenager in 1840s North Carolina. The lad was tending the smouldering fire that produced smoke for a tobacco-curing barn. He fell asleep, and when he awoke found the fire was out. Knowing that this could get him in trouble, he went to the blacksmith's forge and got burning logs to revive the fire. These produced hotter smoke than the tobacco required, and the leaves turned yellow and cured in two days, instead of the usual couple of weeks.

The story goes that the mistake led to various experiments by local tobacco farmers. The end result was Bright Leaf tobacco, which changed the world of smoking. Bright Leaf is milder and more pleasant than the darker tobaccos, and became the sought-after product for cigarettes.

Still, there was the problem of cutting and mincing the tobacco leaves to produce finer pieces of tobacco that could be easily rolled into paper. Doing it by hand was time-consuming. Getting minced tobacco into the hands of rollers became faster in the 1870s when Albert Pease of Dayton, Ohio, invented a machine for chopping tobacco leaves for cigarettes, but that was still only part of the solution.

Back then, a cigarette factory was a place where workers sat around tables, rolled tobacco in fine paper, sealed the product with paste, then packaged it into various forms for distribution and sale. No matter how quickly and expertly the rollers worked, the number of cigarettes they could produce each day was limited. And, of course, the workers had to be paid for their labour.

James Albert Bonsack of Roanoke County, Virginia, changed all that. The Allan and Ginter Tobacco company of Richmond, Virgina, was offering a $75,000 prize for the invention of a workable cigarette-rolling machine. Bonsack, who was still a student at the time, left school on hearing of the offer. He worked on building the machine, and in 1880, when he was just twenty, he was awarded the prize. The machine was destroyed in a fire, and history leaves it uncertain whether young Bonsack actually collected the monetary prize. He did build a new machine, however.

His machine was not totally reliable and most tobacco companies refused to buy it. Bonsack, however, was granted a U.S. patent for his machine, which took in prepared tobacco onto a continuous sheet of paper, rolled it, pasted it and cut it into cigarette lengths. The machine could make 120,000 cigarettes a day — far more than a room full of human cigarette rollers, and it did not have to be paid an hourly or daily wage.

The Bonsack cigarette-rolling machine, invented in the early 1880s, revolutionized the tobacco industry throughout the world. Before that, cigarettes were hand-rolled by individual artisans who could roll 1,000 or more cigarettes in a day each. Bonsack's machine could make 120,000 cigarettes per day and did not have to be paid an hourly wage.

Bonsack tinkered and improved his machine, and in 1885 sold it to W. Duke Sons and Company, which later became the American Tobacco Company. The purchase of Bonsack's machine launched the cigarette industry.

The Duke company had grown from basically nothing. Washington Duke was born on his parents' North Carolina farm in 1820. He worked with his hands, and after serving in the Confederate Navy against his will in the Civil War, he took to farming. He and two sons and a daughter used to beat cured tobacco with sticks, sifting it through wire and packing it into small bags to sell. They also sold handmade cigarettes from their farm in Raleigh, North Carolina.

By 1880, when Bonsack won the invention contest, one of Duke's sons, James "Buck" Duke, was planning how to turn the family business into one specializing in the mass manufacturing of tobacco. He not only bought Bonsack's machine but went into business with him, building a factory that produced ten million cigarettes in the first year. They packaged them in small boxes with baseball cards and called them Duke of Durham. Five years later, their factory turned out one billion cigarettes.

Bonsack and Duke get much of the credit for mass cigarette production, but they were not the first to mechanize the process. Others had been working on cigarette-rolling machines in other parts of the world. In Havana, where tobacco was truly king in the 1800s, Luis Susini, the legendary cigar factory owner, used steam-generated cigarette-rolling equipment as early as 1853. A cigarette-rolling machine capable of producing 3,600 cigarettes an hour was displayed at the Paris World Exhibition in 1867. The Abadie Company of Paris was granted a patent for a cigarette-rolling machine in 1874.

However, Bonsack's improved machinery became the most used. His machine, and the vision and drive of the Duke family, made the cigarette the dominant tobacco product throughout the world. Machines began producing billions of cigarettes quickly and cheaply.

The cigarette was the long-sought "beautiful delivery system." It put nicotine quickly into the bloodstream, was easily portable, and readily available for prices well within the reach of most people. The fast growth in its popularity can be seen in U.S. government-revenue reports. Cigarettes taxes were 13.6 percent of U.S. federal tobacco revenue in 1910. Ten years later they were 51.1 percent, and by 1971, they accounted for a whopping 97.2 percent of all tobacco revenues.

The machine-produced cigarette changed the image of smoking. The cigarette was slim, delicate, and white. It was a clean and sanitary product when compared with a soggy cigar end, the yellowed, tobacco juice-stained lips produced by chewing tobacco, or the messy business of pipe use. The relative cleanliness and alluring look of the cigarette helped to make smoking attractive to women.

The growing popularity of cigarettes caught the bold and probing eyes of government accountants and politicians. Cigarettes became a prime source of tax revenue. Governments saw these addictive items as the perfect means of acquiring more funds to pay for the increasing demands of their citizens, and, of course, to pay for wars.

9

Tobacco and Bullets

Wars favoured the tobacco industry. Combat built a bond between discomfited soldiers and tobacco's soothing nicotine. Nicotine steadied the soldier's shaking hands, eased his hunger and pain, relieved his stress, and brought him closer to his band of brothers.

Tobacco became the European soldier's friend soon after the Spanish conquistadors began conquering the Indians of the Americas. It befriended the sailors plying the Atlantic between Europe and the New World. It went with the troops into battles between the nations in Europe, and later into the battles of people against each other in the Americas.

Tobacco was a major factor in the American Revolutionary War against Britain. Tobacco exports, well over one hundred million pounds a year just before the war, constituted one-half of all the export trade with Britain. Tobacco farmers along Chesapeake Bay, also known as the Tobacco Coast, were fed up with regularly being in debt to British merchants, and heavily taxed by the British Crown. The rebelling colonies helped finance the Revolutionary War, also known in some areas as "the Tobacco War," by using five million pounds of Virginia tobacco as collateral for a loan from France. George Washington, commander of the Revolutionary Army and a tobacco farmer, urged the breakaway citizenry to support and supply his troops. "If you can't send money, send tobacco," he appealed.

Some of those who did not support him and the revolution fled north into Canada, taking with them tobacco seeds and cultivation skills.

The Crimean War of 1853 to 1856 gave tobacco a boost among the British and French. It was a dirty, miserable war, started when Russia occupied parts of the Crimea previously held by Turkey. Britain and France opposed Russia's action and declared war against it. The war became known as the first "modern" war because of the use of such new inventions as the railway and the telegraph. It is also famous for the pioneering nursing work of women like Florence Nightingale.

Nightingale and other nurses found conditions among Britain's wounded soldiers intolerable. Conditions in battlefield hospitals were filthy, and there was a lack of supplies to keep them clean. The wounded arrived in dirty, bloody clothes that had not been changed in two months and were "literally crawling" with bugs and germs. Nightingale campaigned for reforms that would allow soldiers to be treated in clean, well-supplied army hospitals, which would lower the high death rate caused by the poor conditions.

Nightingale also spoke in favour of allowing soldiers to smoke. "Tobacco is, above all, the luxury which the soldier most enjoys and far be it from me to grudge it him in this miserable war," Nightingale wrote in one of her famous letters from the Crimea.

Nightingale's campaign for better conditions and treatment of the wounded caught the attention of people back in Britain. Before the war the British upper class had considered cigarette smoking as a low-class, vulgar habit. Cigarette tobacco was considered weak-tasting and using it was unmanly. Common soldiers and sailors smoked cigarettes occasionally, however, to show they were daredevil men of the world who didn't care what others thought.

British and French veterans brought back the cigarette habit from their Turkish allies. The Turks had cultivated their own blends of tobacco and had adopted the practice of rolling it in paper. Crimea veterans were viewed as respected war heroes, and their cigarette smoking habits became fashionable.

Philip Morris, who operated a tobacco shop in London's Bond Street, picked up on the trend brought back from the Crimea and catered to it. Some historians believe that the Crimean War marked the introduction of the cigarette habit into Britain.

Five years after the Crimean War ended, tobacco history took another important turn when Americans went to war against each other. Tobacco production dropped greatly during the U.S. Civil War (1861–65). That war disrupted tobacco growing and production. Tobacco warehouses were turned into prisons. The Confederacy pleaded with its people to stop tobacco production in favour of growing food and producing war materials. Fewer tobacco products were available for the general public, but soldiers on the two sides did not suffer from tobacco shortages. As a result tobacco use increased and cigarettes became more popular, prompting the efforts of entrepreneurs such as the Dukes to build up their cigarette businesses.

For years before the Civil War, the U.S. Navy had included tobacco in the rations of its sailors. The Confederate Army decided to do the same for its troops partway through the war. Thousands of Northern soldiers were introduced to tobacco during campaigns into the tobacco-producing South. During battlefield lulls, Union and Confederate soldiers sometimes exchanged foodstuffs and other necessities or comforts. Typically, Union soldiers offered Northern coffee in exchange for Southern tobacco products. Later, Union soldiers raided fields and warehouses and discovered the mild sweetness of Southern Bright Leaf tobacco. The war helped Bright Leaf and cigarettes catch on with the Northern public.

The importance of tobacco to soldiers was seen in a memo issued by the Army of Tennessee in July 1861:

General Order No. 29.
Headquarters, Army of Tennessee, Memphis,
July 24, 1861

The use of tobacco having become so fixed a habit with a very large proportion of our troops that the deprivation of it is to them a very severe inconvenience, and it being impossible for them to procure it at many of the encampments, the Major-General commanding, after consultation with and with the approval of his excellency, the Governor of the State, directs the various Commissary Staffs throughout the State to purchase by wholesale, from time to time, such amounts of good tobacco as may be necessary, and resell it to the soldiers of the Army of Tennessee at the cost price.

By command of Major-General, Gideon J. Pillow, Commanding the Army of Tennessee.

Tobacco use during the Civil War also revealed distinctions between social classes. Officers, such as Northern General William Tecumseh Sherman, smoked cigars, while enlisted men chewed tobacco plugs or smoked pipes and rough-rolled cigarettes.

By the time it ended, the U.S. Civil War had done much to advance addictions. Nicotine and coffee were the soldiers' comfort. For those unfortunate enough to be wounded or sick, a third addiction became available: narcotics. Morphine was used generously by medical staff during the conflict and doctors handed out opium pills to soldiers like candy on Halloween. It is believed that tens of thousands of soldiers developed narcotics addictions during that war.

When the First World War started, there was little concern about addictions to tobacco, or coffee. The public understood that tobacco was an important requirement for soldiers in the trenches. This attitude was perfectly communicated in *The Maple Leaf*, the magazine for the Canadian forces: "In this war, at any rate, they march all the better when they have a cigarette between their teeth...."

People across Canada raised funds to buy tobacco for the boys on the European front. Below are a couple of examples:

- the *Cariboo Observer*, in Quesnel, B.C., promoted in its February 3, 1917, issue a "Masquerade Ball" to raise funds for troops. "It costs nearly $50 to supply the boys at the front with tobacco twice a month," said the newspaper promotion. Ladies were charged $0.50 admission to the ball, men $0.75;
- the *Toronto World* of September 13, 1915, showed an advertisement for the Over-Seas Club Tobacco Fund, noting that "$0.25 means a whole week's smokes," and "five packages or 50 good cigarettes to make trench life endurable."

Many soldiers routinely smoked fifty cigarettes a day.

The importance of cigarettes to the First World War soldier was described by an Ottawa doctor, Lieutenant-Colonel F. McKelvey Bell: "For him the cigarette is the panacea for all ills. I have seen men die with a cigarette between their lips — the last favour they had requested on earth. If the soldier is in pain, he smokes for comfort. When he receives good news, he smokes for joy; if the news is bad, he smokes for consolation; if he is well — he smokes. But good news or bad, sick or well, he always smokes."

Lieutenant-Colonel Bell described the arrival of a train of wounded men in France. One tall, pale-looking youngster was standing with one arm in his coat. He saluted with his other hand

and asked for help lighting a match. He explained that he had had his hand blown off that morning. Bell was taken aback and said he must be in pain.

"It does give me 'Gip' now and then. I can bear it better when I smoke," the soldier replied.

Some American military leaders felt that tobacco was a critical supply for soldiers. General John J. (Black Jack) Pershing, commander of American Expeditionary Force in Europe, was quoted as saying: "You ask what we need to win this war. I answer tobacco, as much as bullets. Tobacco is as indispensable as the daily ration. We must have thousands of tons of it without delay."

Someone was listening because at one point the U.S. War Department bought the entire output of the Bull Durham Tobacco Company in North Carolina.

German soldiers in the First World War also received tobacco in their daily rations, with a choice of two cigars, two cigarettes, an ounce of pipe tobacco, or a small amount of chewing tobacco or snuff.

Tobacco did more for soldiers than calm their nerves, ease their pain and hunger, and provide social activity to ward off boredom. It sometimes saved lives. During the First World War, soldiers sometimes did not know when they had been gassed. Then it was discovered that if a soldier was unknowingly exposed to gas and then smoked or chewed tobacco, the smoke or juice tasted acrid. This alerted others so that medical help could be got before the soldier's lungs filled with fluid.

First World War trench warfare possibly was the birthplace of the superstition that it is very unlucky to light three cigarettes from one match. The popular belief was that an enemy sniper would use the light made by a match to locate a target. If the match was kept lit for the time necessary to light for three cigarettes, the sniper had time to take good aim and fire.

Soldiers with cigarettes became an iconic image through the Second World War, along with the wars in Korea and Vietnam. Most people felt that soldiers putting their lives on the lines in combat deserved some comfort, and few, until recent times, raised the issue of health dangers from soldiers smoking.

That changed in 1964, when the U.S. surgeon general released a famous report, *Smoking and Health*, which contained the chilling message that, yes, smoking definitely does cause cancer. That report changed the history of smoking. Close to one-half of North American adults smoked back then. Since that time, however, the numbers have dropped to roughly 20 percent today.

Tobacco rations for Canadian and American troops have been eliminated today. However, smoking rates among military personnel remain higher today than among the general population. Although fewer than one-fifth of Canadians and Americans smoke, about 33 percent of U.S. soldiers smoke. Approximately one-half of the men and women deployed to Iraq smoked.

A study of U.S. soldiers who served in Iraq and Afghanistan found that smoking during those deployments was considered normal behaviour. The study found, too, that soldiers felt smoking improved job performance and reduced boredom. Also, cigarettes were used to stay awake during long missions. Soldiers said smoking reduced stress and took their minds off being in a horrid place. Such statements closely resemble those of soldiers from the past. One change was noted, however: only smokeless tobacco was allowed during patrols and night missions in Iraq and Afghanistan.

Camaraderie was given as another reason for smoking. Designated smoking areas were seen as popular places for sharing information. "I smoked primarily as a way to maintain communication," said one of the soldiers in the study. "The best way to get information and disseminate it was smoking areas," said a commander. Some veterans said smoking was a reason to gather and offer silent support after a comrade was killed in action. "We'd know one of the guys didn't come back and we'd all sit there and smoke and nobody would say a word."

Many soldiers continued to smoke when returned home, even though they wanted to quit. They cited combat injuries, unstructured life outside the military, and hypervigilance for their continued smoking, and admitted that smoking was also a physical addiction.

Bans on smoking in the military have been discussed. There are already a variety of restrictions in place, including indoor smoking bans on military bases, and prohibition during basic training. Cessation help is available and encouraged, but military culture still sees smoking as the soldier's right.

Interestingly, there was a prominent voice against tobacco use among soldiers during the Second World War, and it came from an unexpected place: Nazi Germany. Adolf Hitler, a reformed smoker who once smoked up to forty cigarettes a day, said it was a mistake to give German soldiers free cigarettes. According to Hitler, "It was a mistake, traceable to the army leadership at the time, to have started giving our soldiers daily rations of tobacco at the beginning of the war."

Hitler's views were part of a Nazi anti-tobacco campaign that included limiting tobacco rations for soldiers, holding lectures to inform soldiers about basic medical issues, and introducing smoking bans in some work places and on public transportation. Given his views, Hitler would not have been impressed with a 2008 report on the state of the new German army. A government study showed that 70 percent of German soldiers were heavy smokers, and 40 percent were overweight.

Reinhold Robbe, then-German army ombudsman, who coordinated the study, said: "Plainly put, the soldiers are too fat, do too little sport, and take little care of their diet. The revelations are alarming."

That fact would have angered Hitler; it is likely, too, that the man who called tobacco "the wrath of the Red Man against the white man, vengeance for having been given hard liquor," certainly would not have been amused by the fact that the modern German army receives its cigarette supplies from Canadian Indians. In 2006, Grand River Enterprises of Six Nations Reserve outside Brantford, Ontario, began supplying cigarettes to the German army from a modern plant it built in Brandenburg.

10

Taxation

Wars that nourished tobacco use had to be paid for, and governments saw quickly that taxing tobacco was a way to finance the costs of war. Raising money to pay for war was not the first reason for taxing tobacco. Taxation and other fiscal burdens were designed first to discourage tobacco use. When these did not eliminate tobacco use, governments looked to taxation revenue to pay its bills, the largest of which resulted from wars.

Today tobacco taxation is an important general revenue tool for governments, who justify it as necessary to help pay the costs of treating smoking-related health problems.

U.S. tobacco taxation for war began with an *ad valorem* tax on cigars in 1862 to finance the mounting costs of the Civil War. The tax was raised in 1864 and applied to cigarettes, which were gaining in popularity. More increases followed in 1865 and 1866. There was a temporary reduction on cigar and cigarette tax following the war, but the Spanish-American War, which began in 1898, created a perceived need for further increases. From then on there was no looking back, and tobacco taxation revenue began finding a permanent place in government ledgers around the world.

Canadian tobacco taxes in some form have existed almost since the beginning. The Sovereign Council in Quebec imposed duties on tobacco in 1670. People avoided them by growing their own tobacco, and by some smuggling. Tobacco taxation continued with British rule but, again, was not effective. After more than one hundred years of British rule, the 1871 census showed that 1.2 million pounds of tobacco were grown in Quebec but that excise tax was collected on only 55,000 pounds of that. The problem was that tobacco leaf was taxed only when it entered a factory for production. Most tobacco never saw a factory door because it was processed at home or in small, unregistered operations. So, the government lost huge amounts of tax on tobacco leaf used for private production.

Along with the attempts to evade taxation, there were also campaigns to reduce or eliminate tobacco taxes. Tobacco manufacturers hated the taxes, of course, because they restricted profit growth. Taxes increased the price to consumers, providing another reason for people to grow their own tobacco and produce their own smoking products.

The Tobacco Association of Canada prepared a lobbying brief in 1876 titled *Serious Loss of Revenue to the Country* that argued tobacco taxation had created an illicit tobacco trade. The association argued that it was up to the government to strictly enforce tax laws, or eliminate tobacco taxes. These are some of the same arguments that the tobacco industry still uses today.

Two years later, in 1878, the issue of abolishing tobacco taxes was debated in the House of Commons. A motion calling for abolishing the taxes said excise taxes were preventing growth of a Canadian tobacco industry. Wilfrid Laurier, then-revenue minister, noted that Canadian conditions were not the best for tobacco growing anyway. The government also argued that tobacco was injurious to health. The motion was defeated.

Canadian tobacco taxes were increased again in 1897, creating more industry anger that resulted in more lobbying against tobacco taxation.

One of the leading lobby groups against tobacco use was the Women's Christian Temperance Union (WCTU), which got its start in Ontario in 1875. Modelled after the U.S. WCTU, it promoted temperance, social purity, and the enfranchisement of women, campaigning vigorously against alcohol and tobacco.

In 1903 it campaigned for a bill in Parliament to outlaw cigarettes. That bill failed because of a technicality, but the WCTU continued its efforts, and did help in getting a law passed prohibiting the sale of tobacco to anyone under sixteen years of age.

The WCTU had much better luck in its U.S. campaigns. The Anti-Cigarette League of America, an offshoot of the WCTU, was popular, and between 1890 and 1935 politicians heard its strident calls and banned the manufacture, sale, and possession of tobacco products in fifteen states.

The anti-tobacco struggle was a difficult one, however, since governments found the revenue generated by taxing tobacco very attractive. It's not difficult to see how government became addicted to tobacco taxes. By 1880 the United States got 31 percent of all its taxes from tobacco. Of that, 50 percent came from chewing and smoking tobacco, 40 percent from cigars, and less than 2 percent from cigarettes, a figure that skyrocketed in the 1900s.

Tobacco taxes expanded and soared worldwide in the early 1900s. They increased 500 percent between 1910 and 1920 alone in the United States. Since then many governments have seen the revenue potential of tobacco taxes, and they have come to be accepted as a means to discourage smoking, and to pay for ever-expanding government services.

Tobacco tax decreases seldom happen. In the United States, Kentucky and Virginia, both leading tobacco producers, are the only two states in history to have reduced cigarette taxes. That was by one-half a cent a pack and occurred more than fifty years ago.

Canada made a famous cigarette tax reduction in 1994 in a desperate effort to end a national contraband-cigarette crisis. The crisis developed after a series of tobacco tax increases, and by 1993 alarm was raised about the increasing violent side effects of cigarette smuggling that previously had little public visibility.

Federal and provincial tobacco taxes had been increased substantially in the late 1980s and early 1990s. These increases, combined with some other factors, spawned an outbreak of cross-border smuggling, diversions, and robberies with violence. It was estimated that the federal and provincial governments were losing $2 billion a year in taxes because of the smuggling. The federal government, spurred on by media attention and the lost revenue, stepped in.

Jean Chrétien, prime minister at the time, said cigarette smuggling was threatening the safety of Canadian communities, and the livelihood of law-abiding merchants. Cigarette smuggling "is a threat to the very fabric of Canadian society," he said.

Chrétien's solicitor general, Herb Gray, added: "Organized crime has become a major player in the contraband cigarette market. What we are seeing is a frightening growth in criminal activity. We are seeing a breakdown in respect for Canadian law. Canadian society is the victim."

That crisis, the events leading up to it, and the aftermath are discussed in more depth in later chapters.

Since that crisis, arguments have raged about the pros and cons of tobacco taxation. Some say higher taxes promote smuggling, while others say there is proof that higher taxation lowers the smoking rates. The World Health Organization (WHO) argues that many smokers now accept, and even support, tobacco taxes because they understand that tobacco use is harmful to health. "Tax increases raise government revenues, which can be used for tobacco control and other important health and social programmes; allocating tax revenues in this way further increases popular support for raising taxes," the WHO says in its 2011 report *The Global Tobacco Epidemic*.

That opinion is reinforced by the International Union Against Tuberculosis and Lung Disease: "The demand for tobacco is strongly influenced by its price. Taxation is the most cost-effective way of reducing tobacco consumption, especially among young people and those on low income. In high-income countries, taxation generates significant revenues for governments. It can also cover the costs to society of tobacco use."

There are opposing views.

"Though taxes are not the only factor enabling the black market for tobacco, the imposition of excessively high taxes on tobacco is likely the main factor encouraging the contraband trade," says the Fraser Institute, a Canadian think-tank promoting free market principles. "Policy makers should recognize the impact that eliminating taxes is likely to have on thwarting the contraband tobacco trade. It is possible that eliminating tobacco excise taxes might affect public health in Canada negatively, but this effect would likely be modest and would be offset in part by the welfare gains from undermining the contraband tobacco trade."

Regardless of what reasons it was started and has continued, regardless of what it does or does not do, taxation of tobacco has become a permanent feature of government budgets. In Canada provincial and federal tobacco taxes raised more than $7.5 billion in 2010–11. The provinces accounted for $4.5 billion, while federal taxes raised more than $3 billion. In 1994, during the smuggling crisis, the total federal-provincial tax take was $3.6 billion, less than half of the 2010–11 figure. These figures do not include provincial and federal sales taxes charged at time of purchase, which add significantly to the totals.

Total worldwide tobacco tax revenue is difficult to calculate precisely. Some estimate the total at $133 billion U.S., just in excise taxes. The exact figure isn't important; all that is important is that the figure is huge — in the hundreds of billions of dollars — and that it will continue to grow steadily as it has over the past 150 years.

Campaigns for higher tobacco taxes have become relentless and will intensify. In 2011 there were twenty-six countries and one territory in which taxes made up 75 percent or more of the retail price of a package of cigarettes. There were another sixty-nine countries in which tax made up 51 to 75 percent of the retail price.

There is growing world support for the two reasons originally put forward for taxing tobacco hundreds of years ago: reducing tobacco use, and raising money for governments.

The WHO, citing various studies, says that each 10 percent increase in the retail price of cigarettes reduces consumption by 4 percent in well-off countries, and by up to 8 percent in low- and middle-income countries. "In terms of demand reduction, increases in tobacco taxes and prices are the most effective measure," Dr. Margaret Chan, WHO director-general, told the United Nations in September 2011. "They not only protect health. They bring in considerable revenue."

The French emperor Napoleon III (1808–73), a dedicated smoker, put the case more directly and succinctly more than 150 years ago. When petitioned to ban tobacco completely, he answered: "This vice brings in one hundred million francs in taxes every year. I will certainly forbid it at once — as soon as you can name a virtue that brings in as much revenue."

11

Smuggling

The earliest tobacco smugglers appreciated the packaging advantages of tobacco and put them to good use. British smugglers used to take one-man lifts of tobacco, wrap them in individual oilskins, and push them off the deck of a ship. The waterproof packages floated on the incoming tide to other smugglers waiting on shore.

Dutch smugglers advanced their techniques by buying presses to compact tobacco and allow more bales to be stored in the holds of a ship.

A classic case study in smuggling — why and how it grows, the extent to which people go to participate in it, and how hard it is to stop — can be found in Germany at the end of the Second World War. Germans were heavy smokers, and although precise surveys were not available, experts have estimated that 80 percent of German males smoked just before the war. The war created shortages; when it ended, imports were almost non-existent because of lack of money, and domestic production was reduced to almost nothing as a result of shortages of fertilizer and farm expertise.

To get cigarettes, Germans had to smuggle them. There were estimates that three to four million cigarettes were smuggled into Germany every month immediately after the war. In Aachem, Germany's westernmost town along the Belgium and Netherlands borders, more than fifty thousand smugglers were caught and registered in 1948, including 4,913 minors. Cigarettes shipped to occupying soldiers went missing and ended up on the black market. Despite the need to smuggle, plus the surprising Nazi anti-tobacco campaign of years before, there is some evidence that smoking actually increased in post-war Germany.

Today the cigarette is the world's most smuggled consumer commodity. An estimated four to five hundred billion are channelled into the black market every year. It's not hard to understand why: potential profits can be astronomical, and the risks if caught are low. Cigarettes are also lightweight and packaged compactly. Cartons or cases are easily lifted and handled. Packed in cubes they occupy little space when loaded into a car, a truck, a van, the front of a motor boat, a semi-trailer, or shipping container.

Smuggling, according to definition, is the conveying of something secretly and illicitly. For practical purposes the word smuggling often is used to include tax evasion, diversion, and counterfeiting, especially in relation to cigarettes.

Smuggling exists usually because goods are prohibited or rationed, cheaper on one side of a border than another, or sometimes because rules covering importing of goods are too complicated. Tax rates that vary from one jurisdiction to another set the table for smugglers. When wide taxation gaps between jurisdictions create an opportunity for significant savings, smugglers organize as groups for making large amounts of money. Making significant profits by evading taxes is the principal driver for organized tobacco smugglers.

Creating contraband profits often creates other crimes. Large amounts of money have to be diverted or concealed. Organized smugglers must find ways to launder money through other businesses.

Also, smugglers use vertical integration, which is the smart business practice of owning and controlling related products and services to maximize profits. Smugglers often include weapons, drugs, and people in smuggled loads. If smuggling cigarettes, there is a great temptation to throw in other items that will make money.

Additional crimes are created by smuggling competition — warehouse robberies, hijackings, turf enforcement through violence.

Cigarettes are a legal product and among the most heavily taxed of consumer products. In Canada more than half of the price of a package of cigarettes is tax. In some countries taxes are as high as 70 or 80 percent of the price. Anyone who can find ways around the taxes is virtually guaranteed huge profits. Transportation and reselling expenses are the only costs, plus perhaps any penalties that might be levied if the smuggler is caught.

Other heavily taxed products, such as gasoline and alcohol, are not that easy to handle. Both are far more valuable than cigarettes, but their profit/weight ratio is far less attractive than that of cigarettes.

A package of twenty Canadian cigarettes weighs only thirty grams and sells for roughly $10 retail, including taxes. A master case of fifty cartons weighs fifteen kilograms, still light enough for one person to lift. Yet it contains ten thousand cigarettes, which would sell legally for between $4,000 and $5,000, far more than a portable container of gasoline or a couple of cases of booze would fetch.

A standard shipping container holds 47,500 cartons or 475,000 packs of cigarettes. The average Canadian retail price of a carton of cigarettes in 2012 was $91 (roughly $55 in the United States), so the retail value of one container would be roughly $4 million Canadian. Profit from smuggling: roughly $2 million if you can evade all the taxes, which are approximately 50 percent of retail price.

It's not difficult to find recent news reports telling of contraband cigarette operations that moved tens of millions of cigarettes involving many millions of dollars. The numbers are often so large that they seem astonishing. Two examples from two different continents in late 2011 serve to illustrate the scope of the trade:

- A large, organized cigarette-smuggling ring that bought cigarettes in low-tax states and resold them in high-tax states was arrested on the U.S. East Coast. Sixteen people were named in a ninety-six-page indictment describing how the operation returned millions of dollars profit for the ring.

  Undercover officers sold about $21 million worth of untaxed cigarettes to the ring in an elaborate sting operation that stretched over three years. Cigarettes were bought in Virginia, a low-tax state, and carried in rental trucks to South Carolina, New York, and Pennsylvania, where the prices of taxed cigarettes are much higher. The indictments described how undercover officers were paid with bags containing hundreds of thousands of dollars, luxury cars, and even a red-velvet bag containing a ten-ounce gold bar. Officials said the resold cigarettes likely returned double what the ring paid for them.

- In Britain, Revenue & Customs officers seized 16.5 million illegal cigarettes just before Christmas. The cigarettes had been imported as fruit, and oranges and kiwis were used as a "cover load." Officials said the cigarettes represented £3.8 million ($6 million Canadian) in lost duty and taxes.

  "Tobacco smuggling on this scale isn't about cheap cigarettes," said Mike O'Grady, an assistant director for British Revenue & Customs. "It is organised fraud on a global scale, encouraging and supporting criminality within our communities, and robbing taxpayers of millions each year in unpaid duty and VAT [Value Added Tax]. HMRC [Revenue & Customs] teams operate across the North West to disrupt this illicit trade, which has a devastating impact on legitimate retailers having to compete against crime on this scale, particularly at Christmas, one of the busiest times of year."

In the United Kingdom the illicit market share is estimated at 12 percent for cigarettes and 48 percent for hand-rolling tobacco.

The Revenue & Customs report of this seizure revealed a bit of British ingenuity in dealing with contraband. It noted that the seized cigarettes will be recycled as fuel pellets for the national electricity grid. One ton of tobacco shredded for fuel is said to light a 100-watt bulb for eighteen months. Seized alcohol is made into farm-animal feed, which must make for some interesting barnyard scenes.

Large-scale smuggling often involves diverting cigarettes in transit between countries. Taxes are temporarily suspended on goods in transit — moving from one country through a second but destined for a third. Exploiting lax transit security and soft surveillance areas, smugglers divert cigarettes to where they can sell them completely free of taxes.

Internet sales can also involve evasion of cigarette taxes. Sellers will offer cigarettes from low-tax jurisdictions, untaxed cigarettes, or even counterfeit cigarettes.

Counterfeit cigarette production has expanded rapidly. High-tech printers and scanners make it easy to produce look-alike packaging for lower-quality cigarettes so that they can be sold as if they were brand-name cigarettes. Counterfeits are believed to make up 15 percent of the world illicit-cigarette trade. They are an especially dangerous product because the buyer does not know what's in them. The European Anti-Fraud Office says that counterfeit cigarettes have 160 percent more tar, 80 percent more nicotine, 133 percent more carbon dioxide, and 600 percent more lead than regular brands.

Cigarette smuggling can be more profitable and less risky than drugs. There is less stigma attached to cigarette smuggling, and legal penalties usually are much lighter. Smuggling drugs means jail time. Smuggling cigarettes usually brings a fine, which can be paid as a cost of doing business. Often, though, the fines are simply ignored.

A convicted cigarette smuggler turned confidential source for the state of New York told a staff member of a congressman that law enforcement is not the smuggler's biggest worry. "Tobacco smugglers' only fear is losing a load of cigarettes," he said. "We do not fear law enforcement. They will pull us over, seize the load, and maybe we get arrested; but most likely not. Worst-case scenario, we go to jail for a couple of months before returning to smuggling again. Think about it. A small fish like me can make $50,000 a month working only a few hours each week. The big fish make hundreds of thousands a week, most of which goes to the Middle East in cash or trade transaction."

Cigarette smuggling fines can be difficult to collect, too, as has been seen in the Cornwall, Ontario, area — the epicentre of Canadian tobacco smuggling. In late 2011 unpaid fines levied for smuggling offences under Ontario's Tobacco Tax Act totalled $13 million in the three counties making up the Cornwall-area smuggling region.

Ontario fines used to be insignificant, but they have been increased so that now they can amount to tens of thousands of dollars, sometimes more than $100,000. However, the smugglers caught are often only the mules: mere transporters getting paid $300 or $400 to get a contraband cigarette load into Canada from the United States. They don't have the money to pay the big fines, nor do they usually have any significant assets that can be turned into cash. It's impossible to get blood from a stone, and giving jail time for unpaid fines jams the jails and costs the government even more money. So, many fines are just written-off.

The mules usually are the disadvantaged and the young, often from underprivileged communities. Smuggling cigarettes offers them possibilities not otherwise available. For a quick run across the border in a boat or pickup truck, a teenager can make $200: good pay for a couple of hours' work.

Jake Swamp, a respected Mohawk leader who died in October 2010, once explained to a newspaper reporter the lure of smuggling to young people at Akwesasne, the St. Lawrence River community that is the focal point of Canada-U.S. cigarette smuggling. "Young people on the reserve are being lured into smuggling with promises of riches in exchange for very little work," he said. "Once they have a wad of bills in their pocket, it's hard to sell them on the concept of an honest day's work for less cash."

For decades it has been the same story: once into smuggling work, it's hard to get out, especially if there is no regular work.

The same applies to communities. Native communities have received tremendous benefits from the cigarette trade, legal or illegal. Cigarette money has provided facilities and services otherwise not possible.

Smuggling is both attractive for those involved in it and very difficult to control. Enforcement against smuggling is fraught with difficulties. Take one border for example: the 8,891-kilometre Canada-U.S. border, which is the world's busiest. Roughly 300,000 people cross it every day, plus 29,000 trucks and141,000 cars and other vehicles. The resources needed for enforcement are huge, and taxpayers often wonder why so many of their dollars are being spent on commodity smuggling.

Law enforcement itself sometimes must question the results of its efforts. Despite government boasts of success, enforcement catches only a small portion of the smuggling that takes place, whether it be drugs, humans, cigarettes, or simply household products bought more cheaply on the other side of a border.

Anyone who questions that statement should look at the many decades of trying to stop the illegal drug trade. Drug addiction, of course, has always been around but it seems more prevalent today. After the Second World War, most high school students in Canada had never heard of drugs. Today police are posted in some high schools and parents worry about whether the drug trade has entered their child's grade school.

Now, more than forty years after U.S. President Richard Nixon declared the war on drugs, some studies show trafficking in drugs has increased. Indeed, Canadian Prime Minister Stephen Harper said in April 2012 that the war on drugs is not working. "I think what everyone believes and agrees with, and to be frank myself, is that the current approach is not working, but it is not clear what we should do," he told reporters following the close of the Summit of the Americas in Cartagena, Columbia.

The United Nations says a global commission on drugs shows worldwide opiate production increased by 35 percent during the 1990s and the first decade of the new millennium. Laundered profits of the narco-trafficking underworld by the "legitimate" financial sector is what kept the banks afloat for years before they finally crashed in 2008, UN drug and crime czar Antonio Maria Costa said in 2009. "Inter-bank loans were funded by money that originated from the drugs trade and other illegal activities.... There were signs that some banks were rescued that way," Costa said in an interview with the *Sunday Observer* newspaper.

Contraband enforcement focuses almost exclusively on the smuggler. The criminals who make millions selling contraband cigarettes would be out of business, however, if there were no buyers.

Millions of people are involved in small forms of tax evasion every day. Smuggling goods is benign in the minds of many. That's because it is considered victimless, and the recipients of smuggled goods get stuff they might not have been able to obtain because of unavailability, or price. Sometimes smuggling is seen as a Robin Hood sort of thing: robbing the government to help the poor.

A 2011 European Union research paper described it this way: "… the stigma normally associated with much criminal activity does not always apply to the ITTP [Illicit Trade in Tobacco Products]. This is because the population frequently does not have full knowledge of the seriousness and consequences of the ITTP and also because tobacco products, contrary to e.g. illicit drugs and firearms, are still considered an everyday commodity, easily accessible to most adult citizens."

Supposedly law-abiding people do it, including those in positions to set good examples for the rest of us. Take the case of the sister-in-law of former U.S. President George W. Bush. Former Florida Governor Jeb Bush's wife failed to declare to U.S. Customs a $19,000 Paris shopping spree in 1999. She had filled out a customs declaration card saying she had spent $500. That's smuggling, but many people don't see it as serious; they don't see it as really smuggling. Dodging taxes is a game for many.

Mrs. Bush was fined $4,100 for bringing goods into the country without declaring them and paying taxes, and had to pay $1,100 in Florida state taxes.

Kostadin Hadzhiivanov, the president of Bulgaria's Belasitsa football club, was arrested in 2008 for smuggling large quantities of cigarettes. He was given a suspended sentence and fined.

People smuggle goods to profit, but sometimes just want to beat "the system" they might see as unfair. We all know that taxes are necessary to pay for the services we receive, but people easily rationalize why it is okay to evade them when they can:

Governments waste tax dollars with poor spending habits and weak controls; governments tax things they shouldn't, like electricity and fuel necessary to keep safe and warm in your own home.

Also, there is the developing view that governments are out of control, spending far more than they take in, building massive debt, and desperately seeking more revenue sources to hold default at bay. The global economic problems of the past few years, and the resulting protests and general unrest among citizens, are evidence of this. Tough economic times and anxiety over the future have toughened dog-eat-dog attitudes, and help the average person rationalize smaller offences as necessary to stay ahead of the game.

The view that smuggling is a victimless crime, grudges against government waste, examples of the famous and the important beating the system, and declining smoking rates all contribute to creating a collective shrug that causes many to say, "What's the big deal?" Those who are addicted, for whom cigarettes are a "must have," are also less likely to see smuggling as a major problem.

Public apathy is slowly changing to concern, however. The National Coalition Against Contraband Tobacco released poll data in 2011 showing that seven in ten Ontario residents are aware of contraband tobacco sales, and have substantial concern about its impacts.

Constant reports of economic struggles in government are making people think about more than government waste. They are hearing more about lost government revenues, especially from cigarette smuggling, and what that money could buy in health care and education and other government services that taxpayers demand. Consumers who bypass the tax system are being seen more and more as depriving others of needed services paid for by the government.

One example of more focus being put on buyers of contraband tobacco is seen in Ontario's 2011 changes to its Tobacco Tax Act. These changes allow police officers to seize illegal cigarettes that are in plain view during the lawful course of their duty. Previously, only Ministry of Revenue officers could seize cigarettes in plain view. This change offers the possibility that more people will be charged for having illegal cigarettes, but is not clear to what extent police will use this new power. If an officer stops someone for speeding and sees a carton of untaxed cigarettes on the seat, will he or she lay a charge? Will those with illegal cigarettes just become better at hiding them? It's impossible to know, but one thing is certain: smuggling will continue.

Whatever the methods, the illicit cigarette trade is huge business. The Framework Convention Alliance, an alliance of 350 organizations working on world tobacco control, has estimated that 10.7 percent of annual global cigarettes sales, or six hundred billion cigarettes, are illicit. The Alliance says this represents $40 to $50 billion in revenue losses for governments a year.

The many other organizations fighting illicit tobacco say it works against their efforts to lower smoking rates. They also say it robs governments around the world of tax money that could be used to pay for treating disease attributed to smoking. The WHO estimates that six million people die each year from smoking, and that number will increase to ten million a year by 2030.

While these organizations work their numbers and their anti-tobacco messages, smugglers work on more ingenious ways to move contraband. There are no limits to smuggling ingenuity:

- authorities received a tip and decided to check out a funeral cortege moving from a Ukrainian village into Romania. They found cartons and packages of contraband cigarettes hidden inside the coffin;
- along the U.S.-Mexican border, smugglers have been using vehicles with large folding ramps to get over the high border fences designed to stop smuggling. Trucks with catapults

have also been used to fling contraband goods over the fence and into the arms of accomplices waiting on the U.S. side;

- back in 2005, authorities at Stockholm airport caught a woman snake smuggler with seventy-five baby snakes nesting in her bra;
- on the St. Lawrence River, cigarette and drug smugglers have modified the live-fish wells of recreational fishing boats for hiding contraband and currency.

Where there is a will to smuggle, and willing buyers, there is a way to get the goods through.

Some smuggling schemes might be somewhat amusing. Others are not. When big money is involved, smuggling can turn extremely violent. The funny stuff gets replaced by gangsters in camouflage suits and night-vision goggles; by people who carry AK-47s and machine pistols, who intimidate, bribe, burn, and rob to get the job done. All that was seen in Canada during the contraband crisis that began in the late 1980s.

12

Return of the Natives

Underground fires can burn for years, decades even, when they have the right fuel, and the right conditions. Sometimes an underground smoulder burns upwards to near the surface, where a breeze fans the heated compost and it breaks into flame.

That's what happened in the 1960s. Native resentment, burning mostly well below the surface since the final capitulation to white power in the late 1800s, caught a breeze and broke into the open. From the flames emerged a large part of the North American contraband cigarette problem of the past thirty years.

The flames of the 1960s flickered in different places, but were most noticed first in the poorer urban areas of Minneapolis, Minnesota. In the summer of 1968, people from the Minneapolis Indian community gathered at the call of some Indian activists, including George Mitchell, Dennis Banks, and Clyde Bellecourt. They burned with modern resentments over slum housing, lack of jobs, lack of proper health-care access, and outright racism. And, of course, ancient resentment over the racist treatment and dispossession of their people at the hands of invaders from another continent. From the Minnesota gathering emerged the American Indian Movement (AIM), a revolutionary group that was immediately targeted by law enforcement as an anti-American group to be dealt with ruthlessly.

AIM began as a social movement whose purpose was to lessen the plight of urban Indians trapped in ghettoes. It focused its efforts on health, housing, and education. It organized street patrols to intercept intoxicated Indians before they were jailed by police, and its work resulted in fewer Indians being arrested by police.

AIM grew and initiated, or was involved in, many protests and confrontations, including the nineteen-month occupation of Alcatraz Island that took place between 1969 and 1971. It attracted world attention, as did the seventy-one-day armed standoff at Wounded Knee, South Dakota, in 1973, which involved the FBI and resulted in deaths, woundings, and 1,200 arrests. AIM leaders, on trial for eight months, were acquitted of any wrongdoing.

The occupation of Alcatraz, the former U.S. federal prison in San Francisco Bay, was one of the earliest and most dramatic events in the new era of Red Power. The Bay area had a large urban Indian population because of U.S. government programs aimed at getting Indians off the reservations and into cities. Universities such as the University of California Berkeley and San Francisco State had Native studies programs that attracted relocating Indians. The Civil Rights movement, freedom of speech, and dreams about changing the world were alive and strong in the San Francisco area.

One of the many Indians attracted to the Bay area was Richard Oakes, a Mohawk from Akwesasne. He had been a high steel worker for eleven years when he moved to San Francisco to attend college. He became involved with a group of activist Indians, which later named itself Indians of All Tribes. That group made plans to take over Alcatraz, the island fortress-prison that is a San Francisco landmark.

Alcatraz closed as a federal prison in 1963, and not long after a group of Indians occupied it, claiming it as a treaty right. The occupation was brief, but the idea of taking over Alcatraz and turning it into an Indian university grew among Indian activists.

In November 1969 a flotilla carrying about eighty Indians set out across the bay heading for Alcatraz Island. One version of that day has Oakes and others diving from a boat, swimming to the island, and reclaiming it as Indian land.

Oakes sent a message to the U.S. government saying, "We invite the United States to acknowledge the justice of our claim. The choice now lies with the leaders of the American government — to use violence upon us as before to remove us from our Great Spirit's land, or to institute a real change in its dealing with the American Indian."

Oakes's involvement in the occupation ended after his thirteen-year-old stepdaughter fell down a set of steps on the island and died. However, the occupation lasted nineteen months before the occupiers were removed forcibly. It ignited a fire inside many Indians. It built a sense of pride, and the realization that Indians could emerge from a dead zone and that many things were possible then.

Oakes wrote at one point: "Alcatraz was a place where thousands of people had been imprisoned, some of them Indians. We sensed the spirits of the prisoners. At times it was spooky, but mostly the spirit of mercy was in the air. The spirits were free. They mingled with the spirits of the Indians that came on the island and hoped for a better future."

Three years later, Oakes, then aged thirty, was shot and killed by a YMCA camp manager north of San Francisco. Oakes had set up a toll on the road leading through the Kasia Indian Reservation. There had been previous arguments between the YMCA camp manager, Michael Morgan, and Oakes. Morgan was acquitted in the killing, having said Oakes approached him with a knife.

Oakes's death was a force behind the Trail of Broken Treaties caravan to Washington, D.C., in 1972 and the occupation of the Bureau of Indian Affairs offices there. The Richard Oakes Multicultural Center at San Francisco State University is named in his honour.

Almost two decades later, another Oakes from Akwesasne would enter the media spotlight as a Mohawk activist. Harold Oakes, Richard's cousin, became famous as the warrior known as "Beekeeper" during the armed conflict between Mohawks and the Canadian military at Oka in 1990.

The rise of the American Indian Movement and other elements of the Red Power movement in the 1960s and 1970s brought a renewal of the warrior ethos amongst Native communities, notably among the Iroquois nations. This led to reconstitution of warrior societies. Debates followed — and continue — over whether some of these warrior societies are involved in criminal activities, or whether Native rights actually supersede some activities considered illegal by non-Native society. Many Natives, however, see the warriors like militias: armed groups that protect their societies,

AIM was an Indian awakening and a call to action that was heard in Canada. In 1974, not long after the Wounded Knee standoff, Natives, led by the Ojibwa Warrior Society, occupied Anishnabe Park in the northwestern Ontario town of Kenora. AIM members were present and involved. The occupation was staged to bring attention to abysmal living conditions among Northern Ontario Natives and to gain recognition for Native land and resource rights.

One didn't have look far to see what the Natives were talking about. Up the road from Kenora were the Grassy Narrows and Wabaseemoong (Whitedog) Reserves, where life for the Natives, crushed by non-Native industrial greed, had descended into Hell on earth.

Mercury from the paper mill at Dryden had contaminated the English-Wabigoon River system, destroying the life-giving Native fishing industry and sickening many people with Minamata disease. Loss of income from the collapse of the fishery led to dependence on welfare, which led to increased social problems such as alcoholism, domestic violence, suicides, and child neglect. *The Journal of Minamata Studies* reported in 2011 that examinations of 160 persons on the reserves showed that 58.7 percent were still affected by mercury and that 33.7 percent could be diagnosed with Minamata disease.

I visited the reserves several times in the 1970s to report on the plight of the people, and hopefully stir governments into action. Almost fifty years later, the outrage and shame I felt then is brought back by the 2011 Minamata study, plus reports of Third World conditions at Attawapiskat in Northern Ontario, and the many other communities that don't make the news.

How a rich and intelligent nation like Canada can be so incapable, or unwilling, to find solutions to centuries-old Native issues, is beyond my comprehension. As a Canadian, I will carry this shame to my grave.

An end to the Anishnabe Park occupation was finally negotiated but nothing was really resolved. Other disputes, with occupations and blockades, followed: the Moresby Island blockade by Haida in mid-1980s to stop logging on their lands; the 1988–89 Barriere Lake Algonquin blockade of a road through La Vérendrye Wildlife Reserve in Quebec, which brought out the Sûreté du Québec (Quebec provincial police) in riot gear.

The Temagami Anishnabe blockade of the Red Squirrel logging road into the Temagami wilderness; the Oldman River Dam blockade in southern Alberta in 1990, in which shots were fired, and protestor Milton Born with a Tooth was jailed: Native awakenings and fights for lost rights and better conditions in Canada erupted across the country.

Armed standoffs at Oka, Quebec, and Ipperwash, Ontario, in the 1990s drew world attention and chilled governments' tendency to use force against Native occupations. Oka, the most dramatic Indian-non-Indian standoff in modern Canadian history, and

Ipperwash are discussed in a later chapter. Both confrontations resulted from the use of undue force applied out of frustration. Both revealed Canadian society's skimpy knowledge of history and its poor understanding of Native peoples. They also revealed how poor political judgment can harden attitudes that stand in the way of finding thoughtful and creative solutions to differences.

The confrontations and subsequent public inquiries have done little to solve the underlying problems. More standoffs have followed Oka and Ipperwash. At Tyendinaga, a Mohawk territory on Lake Ontario between Toronto and Montreal, there have been standoffs involving a quarry, and at one point the Canadian National Railway line was blockaded. Mohawk activist Shawn Brant has been arrested and jailed more than once for his leadership in the blockades and confrontations.

Violent clashes between New Brunswick Mi'kmaq fishermen and federal fisheries officers and non-Native fishermen occurred in 2000–01. Lobster traps were destroyed or seized, gunfights broke out, and boats were sunk. No one was killed or seriously wounded, but a fisheries officer was hit in the face with a rock.

All of these modern confrontations have deep roots, some going back more than three hundred years. They reveal long-suppressed Native resentment over being dispossessed, then subjected to racism, or completely ignored and left to struggle on their own.

John Borrows, a Canadian Chippewa scholar, explains Aboriginal grievances in a 2005 paper on the history of Crown and Aboriginal occupations: "Canada has not yet adequately settled underlying issues relating to occupation of land," writes Borrows, now a law professor at the University of Minnesota. "Aboriginal peoples have long-standing grievances about non-Aboriginal peoples occupying land and blocking them from using ancient territories and resources. The failure to recognize or affirm this problem is a significant irritant."

He writes at the end of the paper: "It is the position of this paper that unresolved issues involving Aboriginal land and resources result from non-recognition and the failure to affirm Aboriginal occupation. As long as Aboriginal peoples feel that their rights are being denied or inappropriately diminished, they will likely continue to take direct action when they are adversely affected."

Native people were overwhelmed by the unexpected onslaught of Europeans who had little interest or respect in their culture and beliefs. Native warriors and statesmen like Tecumseh, Sitting Bull, and Louis Riel, among many others, tried to push back the onslaught, or least protest for some Native rights. They lost, and those who followed saw hope dissolve into distrust and resentment. What is seldom remembered when Natives protest today is that the actions of the early Europeans in the Americas were also occupations and blockades.

Pent-up resentment and distrust has fuelled the Native sovereignty movement, which now has become enmeshed in contraband tobacco issues.

Native activism began receiving financial support from the birth and growth of commercial Native gambling in the 1980s — something that began decades before. Gambling to spur Native economic development was an idea that grew out of the North American Indian reawakening of the 1960s, which in turn had grown out of the U.S. Civil Rights movement.

Indians in Washington State had been fighting the government over fishing rights for decades. During the 1950s Robert Satiacum of the Puyallup tribe near Tacoma fished illegally to test Native fishing rights in the courts. By the mid-1960s, his public protests had attracted the support of movie stars such as Marlon Brando and Jane Fonda. The fight over fishing rights was successful, and in 1977 Satiacum pushed his campaign for Native rights and economic development further by opening a small casino and tax-free smoke shack on Indian land. The U.S. federal government shut him down in 1978, pursuing him relentlessly. He was convicted of racketeering and charges related to contraband tobacco, but fled to British Columbia to escape prison.

He was captured in Canada in 1983, but Canada granted him political refugee status, although that decision was reversed by the courts. He was later arrested and convicted of fondling a ten-year-old girl in Canada but died at the age sixty-two before he could be deported.

Some Puyallups argued that the government was determined to destroy Satiacum because he was a persistent and successful activist. They believed that even the molestation charge was contrived, and back in 2005 said they had a letter from the girl, then a grown woman, saying she had lied about Satiacum touching her.

Native rights issues received stunning support from the United States Supreme Court in 1976 in a ruling that had huge implications aiding development of a tobacco trade and gambling on Indian lands. The court heard an appeal from a Minnesota Chippewa couple who received a county tax bill for their mobile home, which sat on Indian land. They refused to pay and fought the bill with legal aid lawyers. The Supreme Court ruled that a state did not have the right to tax the property of an Indian living on tribal land.

Soon after that ruling, high-stakes bingo on Indian reserves became popular, attracting attention and dollars. More and more gaming facilities appeared on reserves; then, in 1988, the United States Congress passed the Indian Gaming Regulatory Act, in the hope of encouraging economic development and stronger tribal governments.

Gaming on U.S. Indian lands took in roughly $100 million in 1985, growing to $16.5 billion in 2005, and in 2009 gross revenues hit $26.2 billion. There was another roughly $3 billion brought in by hospitality services offered by Indian gaming facilities.

Money from gaming flowed into impoverished reserves, paying for some much-needed services and facilities, lifting peoples' spirits, and strengthening warrior societies active in protests and occupations. New money paid for warrior society organization, communications equipment, and weapons.

Where there are gambling profits to be reaped, there are criminal elements. Native gambling attracted them. Gambling also created a clash of opinions on whether gambling and cigarette money were beneficial or harmful, or even wanted in the Native communities. Mohawk communities straddling, or close to, the U.S.-Canadian border were among the first to see the changes and controversy brought by gambling and cigarettes.

It's not as if there was no warning about the problems that cigarettes and gambling might bring. In 1978 a committee of the National Tobacco Tax Association warned that the sale of tax-free cigarettes could lead to substantial revenue losses for governments: "Cigarette manufacturers and distributors should be concerned because these tax losses must be made up by increases in other taxes, some of which will inevitably fall upon them.... Even Indian retailers should be concerned, because the consequences of such drastic losses of state tax revenues will inevitably result in more demands for an end to the historical tax immunities which Indians have enjoyed."

The consequences were more than anyone imagined, and no Mohawk community was more affected than Akwesasne.

13

Place of the Partridges

Geographically and politically, Akwesasne is a smuggler's dream of paradise: a place of three borders, sovereignty issues, and a waterway filled with channels, islands, marshes, and secluded bays.

Akwesasne, a Mohawk word that translates to "Land Where the Partridge Drums," straddles the St. Lawrence River, eighty miles southwest of Montreal. New York State and the provinces of Ontario and Quebec each cover pieces of it, but it is Mohawk land, governed by Mohawks. There are two mainland pieces of the territory, both on the south side of the St. Lawrence and split between New York and Quebec. Two of the larger islands are Cornwall Island on the Ontario side, and St. Regis Island on the Quebec side, just offshore from New York State.

It has been a centre of Indian resistance to European takeover for more than 250 years. It has also been a focal point in modern Native power revivals aimed at exerting sovereignty rights and helping Natives recover from injustices initiated by the colonial powers — injustices that remain today.

Mohawks and other tribes for many centuries had used the south shore of the St. Lawrence as hunting and fishing grounds. They travelled from the Mohawk Valley for fishing expeditions at the foot of the rapids near Cornwall Island. The Mohawks are part of the Iroquois culture and language group, as differentiated from the Algonquian language and culture Indians who lived mainly north of the Great Lakes. They were part of the Five Nations Iroquois confederacy that included the Seneca, Oneida, Onondaga, and Cayuga. It became the Six Nations Confederacy early in the 1700s when the Tuscarora were accepted into the group.

Akwesasne became a permanent community in the mid-1750s, when some disputes arose among families at Caughnawaga, now Kahnawake, a Mohawk community just outside Montreal. About 1720, two young white boys from the Tarbell family had been captured in a raid on a Massachusetts community. They were raised as Iroquois and ended up at Kahnawake with families of their own. Differences arose, and the Tarbells and some other families moved west, settling on the land between the St. Regis and Raquette Rivers where they flow into the St. Lawrence. They were joined later by a priest from Kahnawake who established the St. Regis Mission.

The move was not unusual in Indian communities at the time. Differences of opinion often were settled by one group splitting off and settling a new area. This avoided continuing conflicts, but became less and less possible with European colonization. Later, if a group wanted to split off, it found most of the places it wanted to go were occupied by colonists.

This was a time of turmoil as France and Britain fought the Seven Years War, also called the French and Indian Wars (1754–63), for control of Canada. Native villages were wiped out during the wars, and refugees resettled in other settlements. The early population of Akwesasne grew, taking in Abenaki refugees from the village of Odanak when it was attacked and destroyed by Rogers's Rangers, the famous British colonial militia that harassed the French in the New York State region. It also became the home of large numbers of Mohawks who moved up from the Mohawk Valley to escape European encroachment. As Akwesasne grew the people spread out onto the islands in the St. Lawrence and along the shoreline at the St. Regis Mission.

Britain won the war against France, and control of Canada. A little more than a decade later, however, the region was again consumed by battles. The American Revolution changed the face of British North America, and Akwesasne Mohawks found themselves divided on whether to support the British or the American revolutionaries, or to remain neutral. Most sided with Britain. At the end of the war, those who had been living in what is now New York State lost most of their land. Many moved to what is now the Six Nations Reserve on the Grand River, just beyond the far west end of Lake Ontario. Those who remained in Akwesasne found themselves in a reserve divided by a British Canada-U.S. border. This border has never been recognized by them, however, because the Mohawks consider themselves a separate nation.

Akwesasne has roughly 14,700 acres on the U.S. side, and 7,400 on the Canadian side. The territory consists of three districts: Kaweno:ke (Cornwall Island, Ontario), Kana:takon (St. Regis, Quebec), and Tsi:Snaihne (Snye, New York). Governance of the territories became a political bad dream. It is governed by a council of traditional chiefs, and non-Native-imposed elected councils on each side of the border.

The Mohawks of Akwesasne claim right of free passage across the Canada-U.S. border as confirmed in the Jay Treaty of 1793 between British Canada and the newly formed United States of America. That, they say, includes passage of goods without duties. There has been much legal wrangling over this, but the Mohawks insist on the right to move goods freely across the Canada-U.S. border where it exists in their territory. They cite various agreements and assurances that the border would always be nothing but a line drawn twenty feet above their heads, and would not affect their lives.

Mohawk sovereignty, plus the geography of the area, have made Akwesasne the centre of North America's most popular smuggling route. The Canada-U.S. border east and west of Akwesasne is 85 percent water. The area is a recreational paradise, which makes it perfect for smuggling. In summer smugglers' boats mingle easily with large amounts of commercial marine traffic, pleasure craft, jet skis, and recreational fishing boats. In winter, when the water freezes over, the ice is dotted with ice fishing shacks and snowmobiles. Coves and canals provide places to move about undetected, plus there are many private beaches, docks, and cottages where contraband can be loaded or unloaded with little chance of detection.

Smuggling in the area dates back centuries to the time of the fur trade. The Iroquois positioned themselves along that stretch of the St. Lawrence to intercept fur traders paddling from the western fur grounds to markets in Montreal. They would trade, buy, or steal the furs, divert them south along river systems like the St. Regis, and sell them in the New York area where prices were better.

During U.S. Prohibition (1920–33), illicit liquor flowed south from Montreal and other Canadians locations, and one of the main smuggling passageways was through Akwesasne. Alcohol was smuggled into the United States by the boatload, with Mohawks used as intermediaries to help get the booze to American gangsters, who organized distribution through the U.S. northwest. It was dangerous business, and sometimes bodies were found floating in the St. Lawrence.

After Prohibition, times were relatively stable for Akwesasne. Fishing, hunting, and trapping had declined, but agriculture was reasonably productive. Mohawk men had gained good reputations as quarriers and railway bridge steel workers during the previous century, and found jobs working high steel in the post-Second World War boom.

Then, in 1954, after decades of hesitation, arguing, and false starts, the United States and Canada embarked on the St. Lawrence Seaway project. The project would create a 3,800-kilometre world-class waterway capable of carrying ocean-going ships from the Atlantic to the head of Lake Superior. The major part of the project was the 306 kilometres between Montreal and Lake Ontario in which new locks would lift super ships seventy-five metres above sea level. The Seaway project also would dam the famous Long Sault Rapids just west of Akwesasne for a mammoth power generation system.

One day in the late 1950s, thirty tons of dynamite was ignited, blowing up the last coffer dam in the Seaway project and hurling millions and millions of gallons of backed-up water into the new system. Expanded canals, dams, and flooding changed that part of the St. Lawrence forever. The Long Sault Rapids disappeared, as did nine small communities that were relocated, and water backup behind the dams created what is called Lake St. Lawrence. A total of 6,500 people, some farmers, were relocated. The familiar surroundings and environment that the Mohawks of Akwesasne had known for two hundred years were changed forever.

Ontario Power Generation apologized in 2008 for the "impact" caused by the Seaway power-generation construction. The "impact" included destruction of the Native fishery. The Mohawks had fished the rapids above Akwesasne for generations, taking fish for food and sale with spears and gill nets. Sale of sturgeon and sturgeon eggs to markets in New York State had been lucrative. The rapids disappeared with the Seaway, which deprived the marine life in the area of the richly oxygenated water it depended on.

Kaniatarowanenneh, the Mohawk name for the St. Lawrence, had provided Akwesasne with food, water, recreation and transport. It had also provided paying jobs: the Mohawks were expert boatmen who were sought after for their ability to guide others through the treacherous Long Sault Rapids and the Lachine Rapids at Montreal. The Mohawks had been voyageurs in the fur trade, and their skills on water had been solicited for timber rafting, and exploration expeditions, including the 1885 expedition up the Nile to rescue British General Charles Gordon from a Muslim rebellion.

The Seaway brought prosperity to the Canadian and American sides of the river, but little of it touched Akwesasne. Manufacturing boomed on both sides of the river. Massena, New York, prospered from plants constructed by the Aluminum Company of America, Reynolds Metals, and General Motors. Cornwall, on the Canadian side, had fabric manufacturing, the Domtar paper mill, and Canadian Industries Limited (C.I.L.). Industries also brought pollution, and Akwesasne was in the thick of it.

The islands and mainland portions of Akwesasne are rural, with pastures and farmlands and patches of woods. The land was important for agriculture; indeed, in 1959, just after the Seaway opened, there were close to four hundred cattle grazing on the Cornwall Island portion of the reserve. In 1962 people noticed swelling legs on their cattle, and some animals became lame and unable to stand upright to graze. Chewing was painful and the animals lost teeth. By 1977 only 177 cattle remained.

Ulcerated and deformed fish began to show up. Biologists discovered extremely high levels of toxins in fish and turtles. Pollutants such as fluoride, PCBs, and Mirex came not just from nearby industries but from sources in the St. Lawrence-Great Lakes system far above Akwesasne. Plants were dying, pine trees were sick, and researchers found people had muscle and bone abnormalities, blood pressure problems, and thyroid diseases. There were concerns that pollution had caused birth defects among the people.

Pollution prevented the growing of food or the taking of water to drink. Traditional fishing, hunting, trapping, and gathering opportunities waned. The Seaway changed Mohawk life more than the colonial wars of the eighteenth century. The people found themselves in a pocket of environmental decay, squeezed by growing industrialization. The looming industrial society and the shrinking traditional ways collided, creating upheaval that would tear Mohawk communities and families apart.

Akwesasne, with many of its traditional ways lost, and suffering unemployment and poverty, was ripe for revolution. The rebirth of Native sovereignty, hostility to outside authority, and resentment over past injustices nurtured the revolution. So did the constant bombardment of messages from a materialistic society.

Akwesasne was not the only Mohawk community affected. Kahnawake, downriver and on the river's south side, opposite the island of Montreal, lost land to Seaway flooding and a new canal. Lands guaranteed by treaties vanished. Households had to be relocated. The worst impact was the dissension among the people. The elected band council and the traditional leaders had differing views on aspects of the Seaway, causing the gap between followers of each to widen.

Akwesasne already was a deeply fractured community. The people had to deal with two countries, two federal governments, two provincial and one state government, three different telephone area codes, two wildly different postal systems, plus competing forms of self-government: the Canadian Mohawk Council of Akwesasne, the St. Regis Mohawk Tribal Council, and followers of the traditional Longhouse Mohawk Nation.

Cultural differences also made life more difficult at Akwesasne. The Mohawks not only had their own cultural changes to deal with, they also had to deal with the differing cultures of the English Canadians, the French Canadians, and the Americans of northern New York State.

These complications were enough to stress any society. There also were varying opinions about traditional versus imposed government structure, the role of warrior societies, and dozens of other living issues. Later on-reserve commercial gaming and the selling of untaxed cigarettes and gasoline to non-Natives created further disagreements and tensions.

U.S. Supreme Court decisions in the 1970s and 1980s confirmed reservations as tax-free zones and allowed Native gambling establishments. These opened a new world for Indian communities, most of which were sinking lower during a period of huge change in North American society. Politicians began to see the Robert Satiacum view that Indian gaming held economic development possibilities for reservations living in constant distress from poverty. Economic development, many felt, could help shrink the billions of government dollars directed to reserves for health care, education, and other commitments.

Gaming was always a part of North American Native life. Dice and bowl games had long been popular, with dice carved from bone, or made from stones. Finger games, games with sticks, and guessing games were popular too. Games were played for entertainment, exhibitions of skills, and often for stakes.

The 1987 U.S. ruling that government-recognized tribes could operate gaming facilities made legal what was already happening on some reservations with high-stakes bingo. A year later the U.S. Indian Gaming Regulatory Act (IGRA) provided rules for tribes operating bingo parlours and casinos.

Canada also moved to allow some Native gaming, but later and more cautiously. Just over a dozen Native casinos now operate in four provinces: Saskatchewan, Manitoba, Ontario, and New Brunswick. The United States in 2010 had 422 Indian gaming operations, earning $26.5 billion in revenue.

High-stakes bingo halls and casinos drew people from outside Indian lands. They came in chartered buses, attracted by big jackpots, and the opportunity to smoke while enjoying themselves. Anti-smoking campaigns had begun to squeeze out the number of places where smoking was allowed, but reserves had no restrictions.

Akwesasne had small-scale tobacco smuggling during the 1970s and early 1980s. It was a natural outgrowth of sovereignty issues. Tax-free cigarettes and gasoline were sold to non-Indians travelling New York's Route 37, which crosses the mainland part of the reservation. It was not a large-scale operation, however, and authorities never got too excited. As more and more people became attracted to bingo, and later other gaming, the business in tax-free goods flourished and attracted more attention. By 1984, well before U.S. or Canadian government acceptance of Indian commercial gaming, Akwesasne had its first high-stakes bingo hall.

Some Akwesasne people did not like what they were seeing, however. There were fears that gambling and tax-free cigarettes and gasoline would bring unwanted outside influences. People feared organized crime, which is regularly linked with gambling operations. Elders and traditionalists said selling tax-free cigarettes was not a proper use of the most sacred of Native plants.

Others, especially the young people, saw it a different way. Out of work, and with jobs hard to find, they were eager recruits to new Native militancy movements. Mohawk youths could draw inspiration, purpose, and strength from the Red Power movement, and homegrown heroes such as Richard Oakes.

As Native militancy increased, so did gambling for profit, and the sale of untaxed gasoline and cigarettes. By 1989 there were seven bingo halls and casinos operating on Akwesasne.

Gaming and tax-free enterprises did bring jobs and money to a land devastated by pollution, poverty, and foreign governance and culture. They also brought organized criminals, more smuggling, and conflicts with Canadian and American authorities. They revealed the greed of individuals seeking to gather as much money as possible while doing very little, and the result was corruption, killings, gunfights, hijackings, and a people confused and frightened.

The Seaway, a gargantuan industrial development along both sides of the St. Lawrence, the evaporation of traditional lifestyles, the Red Power movement, and the money opportunities of gambling and selling untaxed commodities all set up a cataclysmic collision within Mohawk society, a collision that exploded into civil war at Akwesasne.

14

Rotiskenrake':te

The English, French, and Dutch colonists who settled in North America understood war as a natural part of life. For the colonists, war was a civilized and honourable thing, with rules of engagement — spit-and-polish disciplined soldiers lined up in rows shooting at each other. In contrast were the savage battles they fought with near-naked, painted Indian warriors, who rushed about screaming and dancing and tomahawking their opponents when they could.

The "warrior," alternately seen as savage or noble, depending on the viewpoint, is among the most stubbornly persistent colonial stereotypes. Today the Native warrior stereotype has changed — whether Mohawk, Anishnabek, Mi'kmaq, Apache, or Lakota, the warrior is no longer expected to be found semi-nude, with feathers and body paint; instead, he or she wears combat camouflage and defiantly waves an AK-47 instead of a hatchet. It is the colonial image redrawn to fit the modern era — Native warriors fighting over such things as sovereignty issues, land disputes, tobacco, and gambling.

Despite the changes the persistent colonial view of the Native warrior reflects something that has remained constant in mainstream North American culture: fear of difference. With respect to Native culture, it grew from images of wildness, rebellions, and massacres, it was perpetuated by motion pictures and other media, and it has never completely left us.

The stereotype illustrates just how wide a gap still exists in our knowledge and understanding of Native culture. That gap cannot be narrowed without looking at warrior societies within the context of the Natives' overall struggle to save a culture that our larger society does not fully understand.

Warrior cults have emerged in the past forty years as one element of the Native revival aimed at recovering their languages, traditions, and distinct culture. They grew from the Red Power movement, and unlike the American Indian Movement and other such organizations, warrior societies developed in specific Native communities outside the urban centres. They emerged from within and reflected traditional tribal thinking, which is quite different from mainstream, militaristic thinking about warriors or soldiers.

In Mohawk culture, for example, the original warriors, or *Rotiskenrake':te*, were those who carried the burden of peace, those who defended the community when it needed defending. They did not wage war because they preferred a fight and went looking for one. There is much evidence in the confrontations, occupations, and blockades of the past forty years that warrior societies have acted as defenders, not aggressors.

History tells us that warriors went to lengths to avoid large-scale fighting. Tribes in the northern forests of the United States and Canada were not large. All-out wars could quickly diminish populations, so wars were not as common nor as extensive as what the movies portray.

War was not waged with the intent of exterminating another group. Most Indian-to-Indian battles ended without large-scale killing. The prizes of battles were captives, who were taken as replacements for losses. Captives became members of the tribe, adopted sons, daughters, brothers, and husbands, replacing those lost and mourned. The taking of captives was intended as something to help rebuild the society, although some captives were killed under the tradition of an eye for an eye. In Iroquois societies, it was usually the clan mothers who decided the fate of the captives.

There were few fights to the last soldier, and tactics were used to avoid heavy losses. Retreat was a common practice among warriors, even when a battle was being won, a practice based on the theory that warriors who retreat live to fight another day.

The Indian concept of war was changed radically by the Europeans, who pulled Indians into their conflicts and gave them firearms and incentives for fighting. Indian men who once were hunters or builders or religious figures became soldiers of the colonial powers, mercenaries paid with goods, favours, and power.

Indian warfare became more uncontrolled after the arrival of the Europeans and their firearms. Battles involving Indian allies seemed fiercer and more prolonged than had been the case in the traditional, hit-and-run, low-casualty warfare practised prior to the arrival of the Europeans.

It must be admitted that the colonial warrior stereotype developed and was strengthened by the savagery of some Indian groups, particularly the Iroquois. The Iroquois were said to practise cannibalism, but there is evidence they did this to terrify their enemies, in much the same way as they hurled shouts and insults and waved weapons at Champlain in his first encounters with the Iroquois.

Such intimidation and terrorizing tactics were awesomely effective. Colonial army commanders sometimes threatened to unleash their Indian allies on opposing forces who refused to surrender. The threat of course was that the Indians, who the enemy saw as savages controlled by colonial troops, could easily be let loose by their colonial masters and, uncontrolled, the Indians would torture, rape, kill, and plunder. An opposing army under siege had to decide whether to surrender to the protection of the civilized enemy, or risk being torn apart by the savages.

General William Hull, the governor of Michigan and in charge of troops at Fort Detroit during the War of 1812–14, was faced with that decision. He was so terrified of the British not exercising control over the Indians that he surrendered Detroit to General Isaac Brock and the Shawnee war chief Tecumseh without a shot being fired.

Tecumseh was much feared as a savage fighter, but was an example of traditional, reasoned Indian battle attitudes. Surveying the aftermath of the Battle of the Miami in northern Ohio in 1813, he was told that his Indians were torturing and killing captives nearby. He rode to the scene on horseback and demanded a stop to the abuse of the captives, who had been forced to run the gauntlet before being scalped. He demanded of the British general, Henry Procter, why he had not stopped the massacre. Procter replied that the Indians could not be controlled, at which Tecumseh is said to have replied angrily: "Be gone! You are unfit to command; go and put on your petticoats."

The petticoat comment was proven accurate later that year when Procter abandoned Tecumseh along the Thames River near Chatham, Ontario, where pursuing American troops killed the great warrior along with the dream for a pan-Indian movement to halt the colonization of Indian lands.

The modern day warrior cult appeared at Kahnawake in the late 1960s, and was known as "the Singing Society," which evolved into the Mohawk Warrior Society. It attracted young Mohawks inspired by the growing movements asserting Native rights.

A powerful force behind the Kahnawake movement was writer and artist Louis Hall. Born of a Kahnawake mother and Akwesasne father, Hall was a high steel man and had worked on skyscraper construction throughout America. He was educated by the Jesuits at Kahnawake, and in a biography of him written by his niece, she says that he wanted to become a priest, but, a muscular man who liked wrestling and lifting weights, he joked that Roman collars were not made large enough for his neck.

Hall's family was uprooted by the Seaway, when construction through Kahnawake flooded their home. He got involved in legal fights to stop the Seaway but became disillusioned with the Canadian justice system and angry because of the Mohawks' inability to stop the Seaway. He began advocating militant action.

In those days, he and the Mohawk Warrior Society were surrounded by examples of militancy as the Front de libération du Québec (FLQ) tried to gain Quebec independence through intimidation and violence. One FLQ bombing occurred near Kahnawake, and an FLQ sign carrying a proclamation message overlooked the reserve at one time. Taking encouragement from the example of the FLQ and from Hall's urging and coaching, the Mohawk Warrior Society grew more militant and aggressive.

Hall and the militant warriors wanted a purer, more traditional community, and began driving non-Natives, many of them spouses of Mohawks, off the reserve. Kahnawake boiled with tensions that helped to push a Mohawk Warriors Society plan to create a new reserve. In May 1974 they occupied a Girl Scout camp at Moss Lake, New York, in the Adirondacks south of Montreal. Moss Lake was to be a return to the past, a co-operative community free of drugs, alcohol, and non-Native influences. The community, which the Mohawks named *Ganienkeh*, or "land of the flint," issued a manifesto put together by Louis Hall and calling for Ganienkeh to be the "home of the traditional Red man."

"Here the people shall live according to the rules of nature," the manifesto read in part. "Here the Great Law of the Six Nations Iroquois Confederacy shall prevail. The people shall live off the land. The co-op system of economy shall prevail. Instead of the people competing with each other, they shall help and co-operate with each other. Here they shall relearn the superior morality of the ancients."

Ganienkeh began as a community of Mohawk traditionalists, with no band council or elective system. It rejected grants or welfare from state and federal governments. It also became a learning and training centre for the warrior movement in all other Mohawk communities.

The occupation lasted three years, then the Mohawks and state officials negotiated an agreement in which the community was moved to lands at Miner Lake outside Altona, New York, and along the route between Akwesasne and Kahnawake. That community, also named Ganienkeh, remains there today, but is not the pure community envisioned by Hall. It has a bingo hall and golf course, and although recreational drugs and alcohol are forbidden, they are known to exist there.

Ganienkeh came to be seen as an example of successful militancy, an example of change that could be brought about through a strong, militant warrior society. However, five years later, in 1979, an incident at Akwesasne changed Mohawk politics and the direction of the Mohawk Warrior Society, providing a new way forward.

The Raquette Point incident seemed on the surface an ordinary dispute. The St. Regis band council had decided to cut trees for construction of a fence around the reserve. Rival, traditional leaders said the fence would be a symbol that the band was abandoning land claims beyond the reserve boundaries, and tried to stop it.

At the time there was increasing concern about the militancy of the warrior movement. Some Mohawk citizens did not favour the movement's aggressive style, or its tightening connections with people determined to increase high-stakes gambling, and sales of tax-free gasoline, alcohol, and tobacco. Tensions built between the concerned people and those who accepted the changes occurring on the reserve.

The Raquette Point fence dispute became an armed standoff that lasted for just over one year. Members of Mohawk Warrior Society at Ganienkeh were sent in to support the traditionalists. The New York State Police supported the elected council and eventually the conflict created deeper divisions between elected and traditional leadership, and a widening spilt between the warrior society and traditionalists.

New York State finally walked away from the dispute and stopped its regular state police patrols of the U.S. side of Akwesasne. At one point in the Raquette Point troubles, warrior society adherents raided the Akwesasne band police post and held officers hostage. Later, with the state police no longer around, and the band police cautious not to stir up the warriors, corruption and crime crept in.

The band council was taken over by pro-gambling people and the casino business expanded. Gambling halls employed warriors as guards and enforcers. Residents who opposed the changes were intimidated, even threatened with bodily harm or death. Those too vocal about how the reservation was changing would wake in the night to hear bullets from a passing vehicle slamming into their house.

Outside money and influences began turning the image of the Mohawk Warrior Society into something far different from the traditional Rotiskenrake':te. Gambling and tobacco money brought them guns and more power. Tobacco smuggling and drugs and other criminal activities consumed Mohawk life. The communities became board games on which organized criminals manipulated people and events with the corrupting influences of money and power.

Eventually, pushback from inside the communities and law enforcement reduced the influence of the warrior cults. Even some of their earliest and strongest adherents left them.

By then, though, the damage had been done. As seen from outside the Mohawk communities, the warriors had become the AK-47 waving, camo-clad reality of the colonial image that much of the world saw as savage. It was a damaging image that created more misunderstanding about Native people and their culture.

Some elements of the warrior movements did become criminals. They put individual interests, and in some cases the interests of organized crime, ahead of the interests of their own people. Warrior societies, however, need to be viewed in the context of Native people struggling to preserve or recover their culture, their languages, status as nations, and their traditional lands.

Warrior movements are not monolithic, or composed of people who have all the same interests and goals. Some seek the proceeds of criminal activity; some seek self-determination through force, if necessary. Some seek a return to traditional ways. Some seek a Native place within the bigger society. A New York judge captured this in his 2006 *Pyke versus Cuomo* ruling.

Following a violent upheaval at Akwesasne in the 1990s, some members of the community sued the state of New York for not providing them adequate state police protection. Parts of their case rested on the argument that the warriors are a criminal organization that interfered with state police patrols.

Judge Neal McCurn ruled, however, that all warriors were not alike. Some warriors likely even held anti-gambling beliefs:

> The plaintiffs declare that the Warriors are a criminal organization. However, the descriptions and assessments

of the Warriors in the record run the full gamut: young Mohawks who didn't know what they were getting into; traditional Mohawks whose main focus was maintaining the sovereignty of the Mohawk nation; pro-gambling enforcers hired by the operators of illegal casinos; terrorists who wouldn't allow the NYSP to enter the Reservation without the permission of the Warrior leaders; and/or a self-appointed law enforcement entity that protected the vast smuggling operation that was allegedly taking place on the international border, to name a few.

Judge McCurn said that it was conceivable that some of the people complaining about lack of police action were members of the warriors during the upheaval. The point was that individual warriors were just that — individuals with different views and different values, and not a monolithic group marching lockstep to one destination with one purpose.

Whatever they were originally, and whatever they became, and whatever they are now, the warrior cults caught the attention of the public, and served a political purpose for the Indian movement.

15

Civil War

Cigarette smuggling and commercial gambling pushed Akwesasne over the edge but were not the root causes of its descent into civil war. Deep divisions in Akwesasne society had long, historic roots, and were not confined to just that community. Sister Mohawk communities such as Kahnawake, Kanesatake, Tyendinaga, and the Six Nations reserve near Brantford, Ontario, shared the roots, and the problems.

The Mohawks, as part of the Iroquois Confederacy, occupied areas of the St. Lawrence River Valley when the first French explorers arrived in Canada. For reasons not quite understood, they moved south into New York's Mohawk Valley. In 1609, Champlain led a party of French, Algonquin, and Huron in search of the Iroquois south of the St. Lawrence. He found them at the lake he named for himself, and stunned them by felling their chiefs with his arquebus. The Iroquois were routed, and the battle left the Iroquois nations with a long-lasting hatred of the French.

Jesuits, who the Natives called *Black Robes*, later moved into the Mohawk Valley and began attempts to Christianize the Indians. The Jesuits' presence was not welcomed by all, however, and some priests were tortured and killed, and their Indian converts were subjected to scorn. Life among the Mohawks who refused to accept a foreign religion became so difficult for the "Black Robes" and the Christianized Mohawks that the priests moved themselves and their converts to the Jesuit seigneury at Laprairie in the Montreal area.

One of the converts who moved from the Mohawk Valley was a young woman known for her devotion to Christianity. Kateri (Catherine) Tekakwitha (1656–80) has been called the Lily of the Mohawks; she became the Catholic Church's first North American Native saint at a Vatican canonization ceremony in October 2012.

Tekakwitha was born in the Mohawk Valley. She became an orphan when her parents and brother died of smallpox when she was four years old. She suffered but survived smallpox, although the disease left her partially blind and with a scarred face. Her followers believe that when she died at age twenty-four in Kahnawake, her facial scars disappeared. Two Jesuits and others who had gathered at her deathbed testified that her face became unmarked and beautiful at the time of death.

The community formed by the Christian Mohawks who re-established themselves in the Montreal area grew and eventually branched out to form new communities at Akwesasne and Oka-Kanesetake. More moves occurred after the War of 1812, when leaders Joseph Brant and John Deserontyon established Mohawk communities at Six Nations and Tyendinaga on Lake Ontario's Bay of Quinte.

Mohawks and other Indian tribes had played British and French colonial powers one against the other as a means of coping with the invasion of their traditional lands. Both powers needed Indian experience and alliances to survive in the New World. After the wars over North American domination left the British controlling much of the continent, however, the Indians no longer could trade their alliances between the English and French to improve their position.

The American Revolution and the War of 1812–14 between British Canada and the fledging United States further complicated Indian life. Many of those loyal to Britain moved north after 1814, to the established or new Mohawk communities that still exist today in Quebec and Ontario.

American and Canadian governments later imposed non-Native-style government on Indian tribes. The Mohawks resisted, but were forced into new forms of government, which were accepted by some and rejected by others. The split opinions on British-American-style governments over traditional Iroquois government still exist today. Smuggling, disputes over gambling, and numerous other issues and problems can be traced directly back to imposition of non-Native cultures and governance on the Mohawks.

Certainly the imposition of governance often involved trickery and force. Akwesasne, which had British-style government forced on it in 1898–99, offers an example of this.

The Canadian federal government tried to organize elections for a council that would govern Mohawks on the Canadian side of the reserve. The Mohawks refused to participate and clan mothers made clear their opposition in a petition to Ottawa.

In 1899 armed police were sent to the reserve to help an Indian agent conduct elections. Mohawk men disarmed them and had them leave the reserve, while locking up the Indian agent in a schoolhouse. There were threats that the Canadian army would be sent in. The police, however, set a trap. A meeting with chiefs was called on the pretence of discussing stone for a bridge to be built. When the chiefs arrived for the meeting, they were grabbed and cuffed. During the altercation one Mohawk was shot and killed. Fifteen Mohawks, including five chiefs, were arrested and jailed for up to a year before charges were dropped.

An election for the new government was held but the turnout was small, despite attempts to entice potential voters with alcohol.

This incident, plus others over many decades, left Akwesasne with its deeply complicated system of governance. There is an elected council on each side of the Canada-U.S. border that runs through Akwesasne. One deals with the governments of Canada, Ontario, and Quebec for various programs and commitments made to the Indians. The other similarly deals with New York State and the U.S. government. Some Mohawks do not recognize these councils and look to traditional longhouse government represented by the Mohawk Nation Council, which is not officially recognized by governments in the United States or Canada. The three councils often meet to try to sort out agreements on areas of shared interest.

These councils, and the people they represent, have differing views on gambling and smuggling. Some see gambling as means of bringing in money to improve schooling, health care, and other social services. Others see it bringing crime, drugs, greed, and abandoned principles. Some see cigarette smuggling as an innocent pastime allowable under sovereignty rights. Others see it as the source of greed and violence and a contamination of sacred traditions.

The Mohawk government at Akwesasne was approached in 1986 to license tobacco sales and commercial gambling. That was when elders expressed concern about marketing the sacred plant, and others worried about the criminal influences of gambling. A committee was formed to explore the issues, and the three Akwesasne councils placed a moratorium on tobacco imports until the issues were examined. However, some people pushed ahead without approval, and the anti and pro factions hardened their positions and grew farther apart.

This bubbling pot boiled over in the late 1980s as gambling operations and cigarette smuggling grew and brought in more money, and more arguments. Criminal elements, predicted by the traditionalists, appeared and included a cocaine ring that is believed to have operated through Akwesasne in the late 1980s.

Angry words between the anti- and pro-gambling factions turned to fist fights and even more severe violence. Families were ripped apart. One woman wrote later that smuggling allowed her aunt and uncle to move from a mobile home to a two-storey house by charging landing fees to cigarette smugglers using their riverside property. On the other side of the coin, her cousin was robbed and killed while making a money drop.

The story of the aunt and uncle was not a rarity. Non-Native organized smugglers were known to have rented, or even bought outright, waterfront cottages that they turned into terminals for smuggled cigarettes.

Akwesasne began to see roving groups of armed militants and gun-enforced blockades. The sound of gunfire became commonplace. Houses of those who made their opposition too vocal were burned. Services were interrupted; school buses stopped running regularly; businesses closed; and more than two thousand people fled the reserve to avoid what, in effect, had become a civil war. Law and order descended into chaos, and no government — Mohawk traditional, non-traditional, or non-Mohawk — seemed able to stop it.

One of the unforgettable images of what happened at Akwesasne was the sight of a New York State Police trooper guarding children waiting to board a school bus.

The climax began on March 23, 1990, when the anti-gambling faction set up four roadblocks to prevent traffic from reaching the casino strip. The gambling supporters responded with violence. Vehicles were smashed, Molotov cocktails were tossed, gunshots rang out, and there was even a report of a bomb being planted on a school bus. There were rumours of hit lists targeting those most vocally opposed to gambling and cigarettes.

By the end of April people were fleeing their homes. Two-thirds of the 3,900 residents on the Canadian side fled Cornwall Island.

Hundreds were given refugee shelter in the Transport Canada Training Institute at Cornwall, Ontario. Roughly one-quarter of the four thousand residents on the American side also fled to different places.

An estimated three to four thousand shots were fired in one gun battle that took place between the Mohawks on April 30 and into May 1. Two Mohawks were killed. An RCMP patrol boat was fired upon.

Doug George, who edited *Akwesasne Notes*, described in a 1991 article in *Peace Magazine* part of his experience during the fighting: "I stayed with my brother, and there were gunshots for four nights straight. We got no sleep. There were snipers around us who would have taken our lives. On Saturday, Sunday, and Monday, a grand flotilla of RCMP boats would come down the river through the middle of the reservation, wave at us, turn around and go back. They *knew* we were taking gunshots. You could hear it in the city of Cornwall. Anybody who lives in Cornwall along the river can tell you it was like a war."

The Canadian armed forces were sent in to support the RCMP and other police forces. More than two hundred soldiers, including infantry and engineers, provided patrols and intelligence gathering. They had electronic warfare assets, a helicopter, boats, rafts, and eighty-one other vehicles. Between May 1 and 3, about five hundred police from six forces had converged on Akwesasne from both sides of the international border. They sealed off the reserve, which fell calm.

The role of the Canadian Forces in the Akwesasne civil war was not heavily publicized. A detailed paper was later written by Canadian historian Timothy Winegard in Volume 11 of *The Journal of Military and Strategic Studies*.

Gradually, Akwesasne life returned to normal. Shelters at Cornwall emptied, schools reopened, and businesses got back to providing services. Sporadic gunfire continued, and although some unmanned roadblocks appeared now and then, they were soon removed. The shooting and burning in the civil war subsided, but the hard feelings over gambling and smuggling did not end.

It was a sad and hurtful war between Mohawk people who held different views on the sacredness of tobacco and the ethics of gambling. While they fought, Mohawks downriver from Akwesasne had started an occupation that threatened to explode into full-blown war, but this time the opponents were the forces of the non-Native government rather than their own people.

16

Police

The presence of police and military was needed to stop the unprecedented lawlessness at Akwesasne, and had been requested by a significant portion of the Mohawk community. The decision to invite in law enforcement, however, was an exceptional step; in most cases, the presence of police in Native communities increases tensions, and sometimes ignites violence.

The relationship between Native communities and law-enforcement agencies in Canada and the United States has often been troubling. There have been many Native–law-enforcement clashes in the past century, but few more illustrative than the crisis at Oka, Quebec, in 1990.

At dawn on July 11, when Sûreté du Québec (SQ) squads arrived at the Mohawk barriers that had been set up blocking Quebec Highway 344 outside the town of Oka and the Kanesetake Mohawk territory, they presented a clear message: *Stop this nonsense. Get the hell out, or we'll start breaking heads.* That message was not sent in those words, but it was made obvious by the vans that contained one hundred armed police in riot gear, and underscored when those officers started lobbing tear gas and percussion grenades into the barricades. Their intent clearly was hostile, even though the Mohawk blockade was a defensive strategy, part of a protest for land claims.

A breeze blew the tear gas back onto the police. Confusion mixed with the tear gas fog. Shots were fired by both the police and the Mohawks, and Marcel Lemay, 31, an SQ corporal, fell and died. The police retreated. It has never been determined whether the officer was hit by a Mohawk bullet, or one from a police weapon.

The SQ storming of the barricades marked the beginning of a seventy-eight-day standoff that appeared to be the start of a full-scale civil uprising. Mohawks from Kahnawake seized Montreal's Mercier Bridge, blocking daily commuters. In response residents of the Montreal suburbs gathered, protested by the thousands, taunted the Mohawks, and pelted their cars with rocks. The Canadian Armed Forces were mobilized again to help suppress the violence.

The Oka Crisis, with its violence and racist demonstrations, was widely reported, laying out before the entire world Canada's failure to peacefully resolve a culture clash, despite its having had five hundred years of experience dealing with indigenous people. Canadian smugness over its supposed superiority in defending human rights took a much-deserved hit.

The famous news photograph of a Canadian soldier in combat gear, and a masked Mohawk warrior, nose to nose, staring each other down, captured perfectly the story of a century of confrontations between two societies. It was a clear indicator that the "Indian problem" left over from colonial days was not going away despite many attempts to bury it beneath assimilation efforts.

The Oka crisis exploded out of a land dispute over plans to expand a golf course onto land the Natives said belonged to them, but government actions to stop the cigarette trade and commercial gambling were at play in the background.

Unlike some other Mohawk communities, Kanesatake in the 1980s and 1990s was not deeply involved in the selling of tax-free tobacco, but there was a bingo operation. In the fall of 1989, while delicate negotiations were underway over the Oka golf course expansion, fifty to seventy-five SQ officers, with helicopter support, raided Kanesatake Riverside Bingo, which the Quebec government apparently saw as a public threat. Seven people were arrested.

Mohawk communities in Quebec and Ontario viewed the raid, and other, similar, police actions against them, as military invasions of their sovereign land ordered by a racist government. Those views were the product of many years of confrontation with authorities over land disputes, fishing and hunting rights, and other issues tied to conflicting views about Native sovereignty.

The bingo raid came only eight months after the sister Mohawk community at Kahnawake received a military-style raid over untaxed cigarettes. In the course of that raid, about two hundred RCMP officers, wearing combat gear and carrying semi-automatic weapons, had descended on Kahnawake. They seized cigarettes and seventeen individuals, including one woman who was pulled from her car by her ankles as she was arriving for work at a smoke shop.

The Mohawks retaliated by dumping heaps of gravel to close roads leading through the reserve and blocked the Mercier Bridge connecting the south shore of the St. Lawrence to the island of Montreal. The blockades ended a day later when authorities agreed to negotiate over the untaxed cigarette issue.

Society generally sees police as good guys, so the public saw these raids as right and proper for upholding the public good. However, the raids raised concerns about police overkill, and highlighted the inability of their political masters to understand Mohawk thinking — something necessary to help them seek solutions.

The Canadian Police Association further inflamed the situation by taking out newspapers ads at the time of Oka calling Mohawk Warriors terrorists.

Governments and police, of course, were concerned about rising militancy among Natives, particularly the strengthening of warrior societies. It was a legitimate concern, but it lacked the perspective and an understanding of what makes Native people different, and why they behave the way they do.

There is a long history in Canada of police being quick to swing batons and fire shots against Natives in non-life threatening incidents. There is an especially strong dislike by Native people of the Quebec provincial police force. Mohawk feelings against the SQ hardened in 1979 when the unarmed David Cross was shot at Kahnawake.

Cross, a 28-year-old steel worker, was pursued by the SQ for speeding and followed to his home on Kahnawake reserve. Cross went into his house, but the police arrested his brother, who had been a passenger in his brother's car. Cross emerged from the house with a pool cue and began smashing the police cruiser windshield. He then tried to pull his brother from the back seat. An SQ officer shot him two or three times in the chest with a .38-calibre hand-gun, killing him.

An inquest ruled that Cross could have been arrested without use of a gun. It accused the officer of abusive use of force. He was charged with manslaughter but later acquitted by a jury. The Quebec police generally stayed clear of Mohawk territory after that, but reserved the right to go in when they thought it necessary.

Quebec is not the only place with a history of shooting unarmed Natives. Manitoba has been in the spotlight for Native shootings in recent years. Winnipeg police shot and killed a Native teenager with a Taser in July 2008. A month later, they shot and killed Craig McDougall, a young Native man, who they said had a knife when they arrived to investigate a dispute in a home. McDougall was the nephew of J.J. Harper, the Native man shot and killed by Winnipeg police after being mistaken for a suspect in a car theft. He was shot while struggling to take a handgun from a police officer.

One of the most prominent cases of a Native being shot by police occurred in 1995 at Ipperwash Provincial Park, just north of Sarnia, Ontario. During a confrontation there, the Ontario Provincial Police (OPP) fatally shot Native protester Dudley George, who was taking part in an occupation of the park.

Like so many others, the Ipperwash occupation had long roots. The Stoney Point First Nation lands in the area had been expropriated under the War Measures Act in 1942 for construction of Camp Ipperwash, an armed forces post. After the war the band tried to get the land back. In 1972 then-Indian Affairs minister Jean Chrétien wrote the Department of National Defence noting that the Stoney Point band had been patient, and if the land was not going to be returned, the band should be offered other lands. Nothing was resolved, however, and from 1993 through 1995 band members began moving back onto the land.

Meanwhile a group of thirty protesters built barricades at the nearby provincial park to reinforce their land claim and to protest the destruction of a burial ground during establishment of Camp Ipperwash. The OPP moved in to remove the protesters from the park. Dudley George, unarmed, was shot during the night police raid. The officer who shot him was convicted of criminal negligence causing death. He was sentenced to two years community service and resigned from the OPP.

The Ipperwash Inquiry into the killing found cultural insensitivity and racism among the OPP, as well as in the actions of then-premier Mike Harris and his government. Inquiry commissioner Justice Sidney Linden found that OPP officers assigned to the Ipperwash occupation made racist comments. Also, he noted OPP officers produced and distributed offensive coffee mugs and racist T-shirts to commemorate OPP actions at Ipperwash.

Photo: Nicole Latulippe, courtesy Union of Ontario Indians

A monument to Dudley George, an unarmed Native protester shot by Ontario Provincial Police in September 1995, now stands in Ipperwash Park just north of Sarnia, Ontario. A public inquiry into the shooting blamed the OPP, then Ontario Premier Mike Harris and the federal government for George's death.

In his report, Justice Linden wrote:

> [P]olice officers have a responsibility to treat all persons fairly and to be free of bias and prejudice. Neither cultural insensitivity nor racism has any place in a police force in a civilized society such as Canada.
>
> Cultural insensitivity and racism do not have a place in the highest offices of the province. Both the Premier and the Minister of Natural Resources made racist comments on September 6 that were offensive and inappropriate in any circumstance and particularly when voiced by the leaders of the province. These views also create a barrier to understanding and did not contribute to resolving Ipperwash peacefully.

The most shocking part of the Ipperwash affair was a videotape showing OPP officers at the scene making racist comments about the Natives. The comments do not deserve to be repeated, but leave the listener wondering how, considering the police attitudes towards to Natives, more didn't get shot.

A research paper written for the Ipperwash Inquiry says that using police in such confrontations "is counterproductive to maintaining order and to achieving justice." The paper, written by Mohawk intellectual Gerald Taiaiake Alfred, and Lana Lowe of the Fort Nelson, B.C., First Nation, further says: "Police agencies should refuse to be instruments in the colonial practice of criminalizing indigenous peoples to create a smokescreen for the systemic injustices and abuses of power committed by politicians. Police agencies should recognize the historical and cultural context of indigenous rights assertions, and demand that governments pursue political solutions to the problems plaguing the relationship between indigenous people and the state."

There was some evidence that OPP supervisors had advised a go-slow approach at Ipperwash, but were pushed ahead by an impatient Harris government.

Individual police officers now receive cultural and sensitivity training. However, the overall law-enforcement system continues to cling to the centuries-old colonial view of Natives as hostiles. Police agencies, notably the RCMP, have tended to criminalize Native protests. That's not because police are not nice people; it's because the governments that direct them continue to fret that Natives are a threat to law, order, and good government.

The RCMP, through its contraband tobacco work, and some of the U.S. police agencies continually try to connect warrior societies with organized crime. No doubt there are organized crime connections between Native gambling and the tobacco trade, but reading news reports and police news releases leave the impression that organized crime has infiltrated all aspects of Native life.

Police often are used as pawns by politicians during Native confrontations. In 2006 when Natives took over part of Caledonia, a small town near Six Nations Reserve, the OPP ignored a court order to remove the protestors, presumably on orders from the top. Ontario's politicians were terrified of igniting another Ipperwash or Oka. When the OPP belatedly tried to move in on the protesters, they backed off and retreated.

A group of residents and business people at Caledonia filed a class action suit against the OPP and the province for failing to protect them and their property. The province settled out of court in 2011, giving the group $20 million in compensation.

The impacts of the justice system on Native people are profound when viewed through incarceration statistics. Almost one-quarter of all Canadians jailed are Natives, even though Natives make up only 3 percent of total population. The rate is higher in some provinces, notably in the West. Native inmates make up 17 percent of the federal prison population, and Native peoples make up more than 60 percent of inmates in some federal prisons on the Prairies.

Official inquiries in the West have confirmed that Natives are jailed more than any other group. It was found that Manitoba Native youths make up 70 percent of people incarcerated, yet Native people are just 14 percent of the provincial population. In Alberta more than one-third of people in jail are Natives. In Saskatchewan Native people are thirty-five times more likely to be jailed than people from the mainstream population. In British Columbia 25 to 30 percent of inmates are Native.

The statistics make it hard not to believe that law-enforcement targets Natives more than any other group.

Most Native people are jailed for property offences, only a small percentage for crimes against persons. Despite the fact that most of the Natives in prison are there for relatively minor offences, studies have found that more than 90 percent of youths in program alternatives to jail are *not* Natives, suggesting a reluctance of the justice system to avoid incarceration of Natives.

The Supreme Court of Canada, the Royal Commission on Aboriginal Peoples, the federal Office of the Auditor General, and Corrections Canada itself all have called the filling of jails with Natives a national disgrace.

Racism against Indians also exists in the U.S. justice system, but manifests itself in a different way. The FBI and the federal Department of Justice are responsible for investigating and prosecuting the most serious crimes on Indian reservations. They decline to prosecute so often, however, that some tribal members have sued the government for declining prosecutions and for sloppy police work.

U.S. government statistics show that charges are laid in only one-half of murder investigations on reservations. The justice department declines to prosecute in two-thirds of all sexual assault cases. Indian women are ten times more likely to be murdered than other American women, and are raped or sexually assaulted at a rate four times the national average.

Statistics are numbers. Personal experience puts faces to statistics. Many years ago I was inside the federal prison in Prince Albert, Saskatchewan, which was built in 1911. I was on a reporting assignment, and as I walked through the ancient building, I noticed a Native man alone at a wooden table. He was staring blankly at a copy of *Fun with Dick and Jane*, the reader that was used in many elementary schools in the 1930s, 1940s, and 1950s.

A guard noticed my interest in the man and filled me in. Natives were segregated from the general population, and this man was having his "education hour." Every time I recall that scene I want to smash something, or somebody. What kind of a system hands a copy of *Dick and Jane* to an illiterate man and leaves him alone to learn to read? Sadly, that's a question that's all-too-easily answered: A justice system that systematically discriminates against Native people.

I hope that doesn't happen anymore, but then I look at the statistics and wonder. Questionable police actions against Native people continue to happen. Late in 2011 a Choctaw living in Akwesasne was given ten days in jail for refusing to give a Virginia State Police officer identification.

Jerry "Leadhorse" Williams was one of several passengers in a van headed for Roanoke County, Virginia, where they were to be extras in a film. State police stopped the van for speeding, and told the passengers to produce identification and to step out of the van. Williams refused. The incident was videotaped and shows the police becoming increasingly angry. Officers threatened to Taser and pepper spray Williams, then brought in a police dog and eventually pulled Williams from the van.

Williams's view was that state police had no jurisdiction over him as a North American Indian. He could have avoided the confrontation by handing over his ID. On the other hand, how many non-Native people, not wearing Mohawk haircuts and riding as passengers, are asked to produce ID and step out of a vehicle stopped for speeding?

Many of these confrontations are rooted in Native frustrations over government failure to fully understand Native positions, or to act vigorously in getting long-lingering issues resolved. The tragic Ipperwash dispute is a clear and uncomplicated example of government not paying serious attention to a Native issue.

Canadian parliamentarians have heard Native voices for many decades, but the problems remain. Kahnawake Grand Chief Michael Delisle asked a parliamentary public safety committee in June 2008 to try consulting with Natives to understand their position in the tobacco industry: "One, there has been no consultation with Kahnawake, which is of paramount importance to any discussions with us, and yet you profile my community relentlessly in the media. Two, the criminalization of my people has to stop. This leads me to state that historically there was recognition of Kahnawake's ability and authority to deal with our people, our land, and our laws. It's time for Canada and Kahnawake to renew our historic relationship so that solutions to these troubling issues can be harmonized between us. In this environment we can expect positive outcomes. The alternative is something we don't wish to consider."

An understanding view of confrontations with Natives comes from an unexpected source: Harry Swain, a former deputy minister of Indian Affairs who was immersed in the Akwesasne and Oka uprisings. Swain, now retired and living in Victoria, had this to say in his book *Oka: A Political Crisis and Its Legacy*: "It can be confidently predicted that similar long-standing disputes . . . will turn virulent. In this post-9/11 world, there will be a temptation to brand the insurgents as terrorists. They are not. There are merely people who did not have the defences, military or microbial, to resist the European onslaught. Their collective grief will not be assuaged, but it can be respected, as can the letter of the historic promises."

Politicians need to rethink the use of combat forces, military or regular police, in confrontations with Natives. Occupations and demonstrations by people who believe they have been treated unfairly require patient and skillful negotiations, not reactions that might escalate emotions and turn violent.

The mortar holding Canada together has always been honest negotiation and thoughtful compromise. Canada has a large reputation as a fair broker of peace. When we bring combat forces out against our own people, we become much smaller in the eyes of the world.

17

Guns and Taxes

Jean Chrétien and his government were pinned between a rock and a hard place in 1993. If the Canadian prime minister had fully unleashed law enforcement against tobacco smuggling, he would have risked a bloodbath between Natives and police. His other choice, lowering tobacco taxes, would knock the guts out of Canada's impressive anti-smoking efforts.

By 1993 roughly two million Canadians were buying their cigarettes on the black market. Chretien's government was losing $1 billion a year in tobacco taxes; the provincial governments were losing another $1 billion. Illegal tobacco had grabbed an estimated 40 percent of the $12 billion Canadian tobacco market.

Much of smuggling was along ancient and well-worn contraband routes between Quebec and Ontario, and New York State. Akwesasne was the epicentre because of its complicated political boundaries and its smuggler-friendly geography. Armed smugglers with high-tech night glasses, camouflage dress, and communications equipment flew back and forth across the St. Lawrence River in fast boats filled with tax-free cigarettes.

Many of the smugglers were Mohawk, from Akwesasne, Kahnawake, and other communities, who were enjoying the game for much-needed fast money, or because their belief in Native sovereignty rights told them they were doing no wrong. Organized crime was soon into the game. Long-established criminal syndicates, Russian and Asian organized crime groups, and biker and street gangs all smelled opportunities for making big money through a hurting community.

The Mohawks were emboldened by the successes of the Red Power movement, notably the standoff at Oka. They knew what everyone else knew: governments now would think long and hard before sending armed law enforcement against Native communities. In fact some Mohawks had warned that sending police into Native territory again would result in bloodbaths.

The situation had become untenable by 1993. Drugs and illegal weapons often travelled among the contraband cigarettes smuggled by organized crime. Rivalries spawned violence. There were also the dangerous animosities that tobacco created between anti-tobacco Mohawks and those who saw tobacco as providing needed economic development, or simply quick and big cash.

Some people had warned that high taxation would create a smuggling crisis. Others had said increasing taxation reduced smoking rates and that enforcement would take care of smuggling.

Canada was riding a wave of tobacco control successes in the late 1980s. Attitudes about smoking had changed after the U.S. surgeon general's 1964 report linking cigarettes and cancer. Even people who enjoyed smoking suspected it probably was a potentially dangerous habit, but they had little hard evidence. When the surgeon general started providing it, serious tobacco control campaigns began.

By the early 1970s, anti-smoking advocates were taking action. Group Against Smoking Pollution (GASP) began as local organizations educating and seeking legislation to limit smoking in public places. Several GASP groups got together in California as the California Group Against Smoking Pollution, which developed into the California Nonsmokers' Rights organization, then Americans for Nonsmokers' Rights (ANR).

In Canada the Non-Smokers' Rights Association (NSRA) was founded in Toronto in 1974 by Rosalee Berlin, a registered nurse whose allergies made her particularly sensitive to second-hand smoke. It began as a small volunteer group dedicated to achieving clean air for non-smokers.

In both countries the anti-smoking lobbies were becoming well developed. The real action began in Canada when a Mennonite politician from Manitoba was made health minister in 1984. Jake Epp, a former high school teacher, pursued tobacco control vigorously.

Just before he arrived in the portfolio a Canadian sports controversy grabbed world attention. The Canadian Ski Association signed a sponsorship agreement in 1983 with RJR-MacDonald Tobacco. There was an uproarious protest from the NSRA, the Canadian Cancer Society, and the association's own medical committee, which included Dr. John Read, the father of Canadian skiing hero Ken Read. He and Steve Podborski, another ski hero, refused to accept awards in the national championships, which had been named the Export 'A' Cup.

The federal government announced that amateur sports organizations receiving tobacco industry funding would not receive federal funding. The Canadian Ski Association ended the sponsorship agreement.

Soon after becoming minister, Epp launched a series of measures designed to increase federal tobacco tax revenue and to discourage smoking. The federal excise tax on tobacco was increased more than 50 percent in 1985; this increase was followed by another bump up in 1986.

In 1987 Epp brought in the Tobacco Products Control Act and the Non-Smokers' Rights Act. These measures banned smoking in all federal buildings and banned tobacco advertising, limited tobacco company sponsorships, and strengthened warnings on cigarette packages.

"Tobacco use is no longer socially acceptable as an activity among Canadians," Epp said in explaining the changes.

The campaigns against tobacco intensified. A federal sales tax of 19 percent was applied to tobacco. Provinces also had increased their taxes, so by the early 1990s the average price of a package of twenty cigarettes in Canada had increased by roughly 160 percent. On June 1, 1991, the average total tax on a pack of twenty cigarettes was $3.72, more than eight times what it was in 1980, and roughly seven times the average in the United States.

So, by the beginning of the 1990s, there was a $3.72 profit per pack of twenty for anyone who could figure out how to get the cigarettes tax-free and sell them tax-free. That amounted to roughly $37 a carton profit; a car trunk or small boat stuffed with untaxed cigarettes would bring profits of many thousands of dollars. A large truckload of smuggled cigarettes sold tax-free would generate profits of hundreds of thousands of dollars.

As potential profits for cigarette smuggling rose steadily through the late 1980s and early 1990s, boats, cars, trucks, and snowmobiles were running more and more cigarettes across the border into Canada. Canoes and kayaks were even used. Thieves broke into confectionary stores to steal cigarettes for the black market. There were hijackings among rival groups and, later, thefts of raw tobacco that could be quickly processed into cigarettes and put onto the illicit market.

Pirates entered the picture, lying in wait for smugglers along the St. Lawrence. They would intercept the boats running the river and rob them at gunpoint of their contraband cigarettes, cash, and weapons.

Cornwall, Ontario, adjacent to Akwesasne and the centre of contraband tobacco enforcement, became known as Dodge City

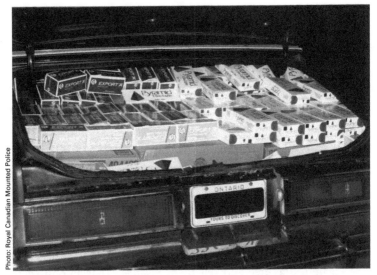

Photo: Royal Canadian Mounted Police

Smugglers use everything from trucks to snowmobiles to transport contraband tobacco. In July 2012, police in the Cornwall, Ontario, area arrested four people transporting forty-one cases of contraband cigarettes in a canoe. A favoured method by small-time smugglers is to pack a van or car trunk with contraband cigarettes.

East in 1993–94. Buildings were bombed, shots were fired into the civic complex, and nightly gunfire could be heard along the river. Then-mayor Ron Martelle wore a flak jacket, and at times went into hiding because of threats on his life. All this was an effort by organized criminals to stop Martelle and others from trying to shut down their lucrative contraband trade.

None of this could have occurred without willing consumers. Smokers saw the deals they made with the smugglers on the growing black market as a victimless tax revolt. It was not victimless, of course. There was a reign of terror during which people were beaten and shot; some even died during the smuggling violence. Some small variety stores went out of business because legal tobacco sales, which drew customers in for other goods, collapsed in the face of competition from the contraband market. Others took to selling contraband under the counter and got themselves in trouble with the law.

Statistics Canada estimated that the Canadian contraband tobacco market, which had been 1 percent of total market share in 1987, soared to 31 percent by the end of 1993. Other estimates give the percentage of contraband ranging from 25 to 40 percent. The situation was the worst in the eastern half of the country: In Ontario it was estimated that roughly one-third of all cigarettes sold were illegal; in Quebec it was two-thirds; in Atlantic Canada it was 40 percent; and in the West 15 percent.

Diversion of untaxed cigarettes for export only was a huge part of crisis of the early 1990s. Some major cigarette companies shipped large amounts of "for export only" cigarettes to the United States. These cigarettes were not subject to the excise levies that applied to cigarettes sold domestically. Theoretically, the cigarettes were to be sold in various U.S. markets, but many were diverted into smuggling operations taking them back to Canada where they could be sold for as much as half the price of legal, taxed cigarettes.

The tobacco companies, meanwhile, lobbied strenuously for tobacco tax reductions because, they claimed, contraband tobacco sales were hurting their domestic sales. Lowering taxes, they said, would stop the contraband trade and increase their domestic sales.

Their export sales, however, had soared into the stratosphere. The number of cigarettes exported, which had been below one billion until 1986, more than doubled in each of 1991 and 1992 and almost doubled again in 1993, reaching an unprecedented seventeen billion cigarettes or 37 percent of total sales.

Later, allegations began circulating that the tobacco industry had participated in the smuggling by exporting cigarettes that they knew would be smuggled back. The allegations led to police investigations, court cases, negotiations, and settlements. Imperial Tobacco Company and Rothmans, Benson and Hedges agreed in

2008 to pay fines and penalties totalling more than $1 billion. In 2010 settlements were completed with JTI-Macdonald Corp. and RJR Reynolds Tobacco Co., bringing the total fines and penalties taken in by Canada to $1.7 billion. The money was to be distributed among the federal, provincial, and territorial governments on a percentage basis worked out by the governments.

The RCMP said the companies pleaded guilty to "aiding persons to sell and be in possession of tobacco manufactured in Canada that was not packed and was not stamped in conformity with the Excise Act and its amendments and Ministerial regulations."

Anti-smoking groups were not thrilled with the 2010 settlement, considering it a "sweetheart deal."

"Canadian governments led by the feds had an opportunity to play hard ball, to build trust among Canadians in the rule of law related to white-collar crime. Instead, they blew away the opportunity to recoup billions of desperately needed lost tax revenues," Garfield Mahood, executive director of the Non-Smokers' Rights Association said.

That settlement was an after-the-fact admission; meanwhile, in 1993–94, Prime Minister Chrétien had to choose an action that would stop the contraband chaos. He considered tough police action, but an estimated 70 percent of the illicit cigarettes were coming through Akwesasne, and Mohawk emotions were burning on a short fuse. An alternative was to cut the cigarette taxes to eliminate the profit gap that was the incentive for smuggling. That would not sit well with the anti-tobacco groups, or the federal government's budget people.

He decided on the latter, and February 8, 1994, became known as Black Tuesday among anti-smoking organizations around the world. He stood in the House of Commons and announced that the federal excise tax on cigarettes would be cut by $5 a carton. Also, the federal government would match dollar for dollar any provincial tax reductions up to $5 a carton. So, the potential excise tax cut would be $10 a carton.

The package of changes also included the re-imposition of an $8-a-carton tax on tobacco exports; a surtax on tobacco manufacturers' profits; an enhanced enforcement program, including more customs inspectors and RCMP anti-smuggling agents; and the launching of a comprehensive anti-smoking advertising campaign.

After these measures, tobacco smuggling activities decreased substantially. The number of exported cigarettes fell from the record seventeen billion in 1993 to seven billion in 1994 and five billion in 1995. The value of exports fell more than $800 million in 1993 to under $200 million in 1994 and 1995.

The long-term effects of the government's tax reductions are still unclear. Statistics Canada reported that the prices of cigarettes fell by an average of 36.6 percent across Canada in 1994, the only reported decline since 1954. The decline was even more precipitous in provinces that matched the federal government's lower taxes.

RCMP and border services seizures, 456,000 cartons in 1994, declined steadily to roughly 29,000 cartons in 2001. The contraband fire was doused, at least temporarily.

Fallout from the tax cuts was substantial. Canada had become a model for other countries seriously wanting to cut smoking rates. Anti-smoking campaigners had argued, and still do, that lower taxes provide young people with easier access to cigarettes and nicotine addiction.

Chrétien argued that success against contraband would restore tobacco tax revenues in a year or so. A couple of years later, federal tobacco taxes were raised a bit in Quebec, Ontario, New Brunswick, Nova Scotia, and Prince Edward Island, and those provinces matched the increase with their own increases. More increases followed a year later.

As the tobacco tax rate rose through the late 1990s and into the new millennium, so did smuggling. Federal contraband cigarettes seizures increased every year, reaching a record 1,079,529 cartons in 2008. Police and politicians argue that toughened laws and better enforcement were responsible for increased seizures. That might be true; however, the increased number of seizures also means there is more contraband tobacco being supplied to the black market.

Canada's Task Force on Illicit Tobacco Products reported that an estimated thirteen billion illegal cigarettes were bought in 2008, up from ten billion a year earlier. It said studies indicate that 30 percent of the tobacco purchased in Canada is illegal. The rates are 40 to 50 percent in Ontario and Quebec, where the contraband smuggling has been most prominent.

18

Rolling Their Own

The cigarette trade with its taxation and contraband issues is complicated. The cigarette itself is not. You don't need the latest high-speed machines controlled by humming high-tech processors with flashing LED lights to make cigarettes. All that's needed is a piece of paper, a pinch of minced tobacco, and steady fingers. That's how the ancient Indians made their smokes, using corn husks, leaves, or reeds before paper was invented.

Ten percent of smokers roll their own cigarettes, using tabletop, electric rolling machines, the old-fashioned band rollers that make a long cigarette that is cut into four or five cigarettes with a razor blade, or even with two fingers and the thumb of each hand like you used to see in the western movies. So, it was inevitable that contraband artists would come up with the idea of making their own cigarettes for the black market. When Canada removed the tax-gap incentive for smuggling manufactured cigarettes, making black-market cigarettes came to be seen as good way to make up for those lost profits.

A bale of tobacco stolen from a farm can be turned into two hundred thousand cigarettes at a small, illegal manufacturing operation set up in a garage or storage shed. The equipment is easily bought on the used market; it can even be stolen. Those two hundred thousand cigarettes when packaged in plastic bags of two hundred and sold for $10 a bag bring in a profit of roughly $10,000.

Photo: Roxanne Ouellette/Royal Canadian Mounted Police

Many contraband cigarettes are sold in plastic bags and are called "rollies." Here an RCMP officer examines a carton of "rollies" seized along the St. Lawrence River.

More of those illegal operations began to appear after the February 1994 tax reduction and the tobacco smuggling controls brought forward by the Canadian government. Those measures knocked the legs out from under tobacco smugglers, judging by contraband seizures reported by the RCMP. During 1994 seizures totalled 456,333 cartons, but from this peak they began a steady six-year decline to 29,000 cartons in 2001. The attractiveness of exporting brand-name, tax-free cigarettes to the United States and smuggling them back had ended.

Small-scale smuggling operations continued with cigarettes stolen from convenience stores, other retail outlets, and from warehouses and shipping vehicles. There were more bold thefts from tobacco farms, especially in the Ontario tobacco-growing region north of Lake Erie. In one case thieves loaded 220 tobacco bales, a riding lawn mower, and some tobacco tools onto a truck and drove off into the darkness. Some farmers installed barn alarms.

After police seizures hit the low in 2001, the pendulum began to swing upward again. There were roughly 39,000 cartons seized in 2002, 59,000 the next year, and 119,000 the year following, and the trend continued ever upward, until seizures topped one million cartons in 2008.

The Canadian federal and provincial governments had made a deal to increase taxes slowly until they got back to pre-1994 levels. The gradual increases grew the profit incentive for smuggling and quickened the cat and mouse game between police and smugglers once again.

Mike Mitchell, Akwesasne's Grand Chief, predicted in 1998 the return of smuggling and organized crime in a letter to the federal government. Mitchell warned Prime Minister Chrétien that tax increases would revive cigarette smuggling and bring back organized crime along with drug and firearms smuggling. He said that jobless Mohawks would be lured into cigarette running, and asked for federal help to develop alternative business initiatives, an international trade zone in the Mohawk territory, and authority to draft local laws to combat smuggling.

"We all know that [organized crime] will use the Akwesasne territory as a corridor for the movement of illicit goods, and that the Canadian government will use the Mohawks of Akwesasne as the scapegoats," he wrote. He said later that Mr. Chrétien and his government did not respond.

Potentially huge profits from discount cigarettes have attracted organized crime groups who take advantage of Native communities and the sensitive land rights and sovereignty issues that exist between Natives and government. The Canadian Criminal Intelligence Service has identified nine hundred organized crime groups across the country, and has said one hundred of these are involved in the contraband tobacco trade.

Early in the new millennium, contraband was back and flowing from the usual sources:

- legal and illegal manufactured tobacco smuggled from the United States;
- unlicensed tobacco manufactured in Canada;
- diverted tax-exempt products;
- counterfeit tobacco products and international brands smuggled from abroad; and
- tobacco products stolen from convenience stores, cargo in transit.

But there now was a new twist. Non-traditional tobacco manufacturing appeared in the mid-2000s and grew quickly.

The Big Three manufacturers — Imperial Tobacco, Rothmans, Benson and Hedges, and JTI-Macdonald — had dominated the Canadian cigarette market. In 2004 their sales accounted for just over 94 percent of the Canadian market. That began to change with the appearance of more non-traditional production.

Non-traditional manufacturing got its start in the late 1990s, when the federal government decided to issue licences to some Native operations. Grand River Enterprises (GRE) at Six Nations

Reserve near Brantford, Ontario, was one of the earliest licensed manufacturers, and is today the largest. How many legal Native cigarette plants are operating in Canada is not known. The federal government will not release the number, citing privacy laws.

Other known legal Native manufacturers are ADL on the Mashteuiatsh reserve near Roberval, Quebec, and the members of the Kahnawake Tobacco Association just south of Montreal. Rainbow Tobacco Company at Kahnawake was licensed by the federal government in 2004, and has become a growing presence in the cigarette trade. It says it employs twenty people at Kahnawake and has expansion plans for western Canada, but is meeting government resistance there. It claims that 1,700 to 2,000 Native people at Kahnawake were employed by the Kahnawake Tobacco Association in 2010. Other unofficial reports say that Kahnawake has sixty tobacco factories employing seven hundred people, and puts $75 million a year into local economy.

The idea of licensing cigarette-manufacturing plants on reserves was to spur some economic development. Native factories would produce cigarettes for smokers on Native reserves across the country, but not for sale outside reserves. Since Natives on reserves are exempt from some taxes, the cigarettes sold for less.

Grand River exports cigarettes to the United States, has a German cigarette operation, and is believed to employ 350 people at Six Nations reserve and another 200 seasonally in tobacco processing operations. It is believed to be the second-largest employer of Native people in Ontario. The largest employer is Casino Rama, the gambling and entertainment centre on the Rama reserve near Orillia.

Grand River continues to expand. In March 2012 it announced a deal to supply China with twelve million pounds of tobacco, which is equivalent to one-quarter of the entire Ontario tobacco crop in 2011. The deal is for three years and could see as much as thirty-five million pounds of GRE tobacco go to China.

The company said the deal will help Ontario tobacco farmers hard hit by government anti-tobacco campaigns. GRE owns Norfolk Leaf, the Simcoe, Ontario, tobacco processing operation formerly called Simcoe Leaf when owned by Universal Tobacco of Richmond, Virginia.

There are no legal cigarette operations on the Canadian side of Akwesasne. However, three factories on the U.S. side are licensed by the St. Regis Tribal Council, which charges a fee on each carton of cigarettes manufactured on the reservation. The council has indicated it makes $4 million a year off this manufacturing, with the money going to a general fund to pay for reservation programs and services.

There are many more cigarette plants operating illegally on Canadian and United States Indian lands. Declining smoking rates in affluent countries make used cigarette-making equipment easy to find and obtain at reasonable prices. Cigarette manufacturing papers and glue can be bought legally in most places.

The RCMP estimates that there are between twenty-five and forty-five illegal manufacturing plants on Native territories in Canada. Also, it estimates that six to twelve illegal operations are active at any given time on the U.S. side of Akwesasne. It estimates that 90 percent of the contraband it seizes is produced on the Saint Regis Reservation. The majority of RCMP contraband tobacco enforcement is focused on routes leading from Akwesasne.

Native manufacturing, legal and illegal, has fertilized the growth of the hundreds of Native smoke shacks seen in Canada and the United States. The RCMP has estimated there are more than 300 smoke shacks in Canada, 125 at Kahnawake alone, and 100 at Six Nations.

Smoking rates on Native reserves are much higher than the national average. More than 50 percent of reserve residents smoke; however, the number of cigarettes produced for sale only on reserves far exceeds the amount that the Native people could smoke. No

Native manufacturing, legal and illegal, has fertilized the growth of the hundreds of Native smoke shacks seen in Canada and the United States. The RCMP has estimated there are more than 300 smoke shacks in Canada, 125 at Kahnawake alone, and 100 at Six Nations.

one argues honestly that smoke shacks are not selling huge numbers of cigarettes to non-Natives. Legal producers say that they cannot control who cigarettes are sold to once they are sent to a reserve.

Smoke shacks sell a two-hundred cigarette baggie for anywhere between $8 and $20; this compares with $65 to $90 for a carton of two hundred cigarettes with taxes applied. For an average smoker, consuming twenty cigarettes a day, the savings from dealing with a Native smoke shop could be in the range of $2,000 a year.

During the 2011 provincial election campaign, Ontario Premier Dalton McGuinty would not commit to cracking down on smoke shacks. He promised to double enforcement against contraband cigarettes, but everyone knew increased enforcement would have nothing to do with smoke shacks on Indian lands. After the Ipperwash tragedy, the Oka crisis, and the other confrontations with Natives, no government was going to tell its police to get tough on Natives.

Two smoke shacks were operating on Ontario government land in Caledonia, near the Six Nations Reserve. The land was owned by a developer who was building a subdivision when Natives occupied it, claiming it was Native land, and that they had never surrendered title to it. Ontario bought the land from the developer to cool tensions and to prevent more confrontations, which had become violent.

Toby Bennett, an elected provincial politician in the area, has been quoted in the media as saying that the government will not take action against the two smoke shacks operating without permission, even though they are on Ontario land. "I've watched it myself many times ... officers astoundingly turning a blind eye to illegal activity," Barrett said. "It's literally right in front of their nose."

There have been reports of people leaving reserves with trunkfuls of cigarettes, which they resell into the black market to turn a profit. The amount of profit to be made doing that depends on whether the cigarettes came from a licensed manufacturer, which pays a federal tax. Cigarettes from unlicensed factories are free of all tax. Profits are also affected by sales tax, however. While most reserves do not collect sales taxes, there are some reserves across Canada legally collecting tax for community improvements.

Some producers, unhappy with the government inaction over smoke shacks, are suing the federal government. One statement of claim says the federal government "knowingly and deliberately" has not collected tax from illegal smoke shacks. The suit, which is a proposed class-action suit and claims $500 million, says: "The Crown agents have ignored flagrant violations of the prohibition on the sale of contraband tobacco products and have permitted open trade in contraband tobacco and tobacco products on First Nation reserves through illegal outlets established off the reserve."

Grand River Enterprises is suing the federal government for $1.5 billion in damages, the amount its Six Nations tobacco operation paid in federal cigarette taxes between 1997 and 2008. It says the federal government has failed to enforce federal tobacco tax laws on reserves.

It's not just cost savings that fuel the contraband market. Access to tobacco is another driver, particularly youth access. The argument is made that since adolescents cannot legally buy cigarettes at any price, contraband markets provide access for a demand that is not linked to taxation issues.

Surveys indicate that most smokers start smoking at some time between the ages of eleven and fifteen. They also show that adolescent smoking has declined in the past ten years. The Centre for Population Health Impact at the University of Waterloo reported in 2011 that 13 percent youth aged fifteen to nineteen smoke cigarettes.

Other studies show that black-market cigarettes attract youth smokers because they are easier to obtain. Surveys have shown that high school students in major cities find contraband tobacco easy, even very easy, to obtain.

The Canadian Convenience Stores Association released a study in 2008 that showed the results of a survey of collected and examined cigarette butts discarded outside 155 high schools in Ontario and Quebec. The study concluded that 36 percent of the butts in Quebec, and 26 percent in Ontario, were untaxed, counterfeit, or foreign brands.

A research paper published in the *Canadian Medical Association Journal* September 2009 found Native manufactured cigarettes accounted for 17.5 percent of all cigarettes smoked by Canadian high school students. The percentages varied by province. Almost 22 percent of Ontario students smoked Native cigarettes, while the figure was 22.4 percent in Quebec. However, in the Prairie provinces only 2.5 percent or less smoked Native cigarettes.

Native tobacco manufacturing is centred in Ontario and Quebec and that's where distribution is heaviest. That is starting to change, however, as Native manufacturers push west, and Native retail outlets are now appearing in Manitoba, Saskatchewan, and Alberta.

Some updated work by the same researchers reported in 2011 that Native-brand cigarettes rose as a percentage of total cigarettes smoked by Ontario high school students from 26 percent in 2006 to 43 percent in 2009. It showed that 73 percent of student smokers in Toronto used contraband cigarettes in the previous month. The percentage in Montreal was 79, and in Ottawa 63. The same study reported that one-third of these young smokers think Native-brand cigarettes are less harmful than fully taxed brands.

A casual conversation with a retired high school principal in Ontario provides another interesting angle on contraband cigarettes and students. She said smoking black-market cigarettes provides youth with cheap entertainment. It might cost a group of friends $25 each to go to a movie. They have to pay for admission, snacks, and transport to and from the theatre. For $10 the group can buy a baggie of two hundred cigarettes and sit around smoking and talking for an entire weekend.

High rates of black-market cigarette smoking by youth are not limited to Canada.

A study of fifteen- and sixteen-year-old students in the northwest of England found that 28 percent purchased "fake cigarettes." Nor is it limited to Western countries. A 2010 study in *The Asian Economic Journal* found that in Taiwan the young, particularly students and low-income people, are most likely to smoke contraband.

While black-market cigarettes increase access for youth, they also make it much harder for the poor to quit smoking. There is little argument that raising cigarette prices is an effective way to lower overall smoking rates. That is a credo now among tobacco control groups, and it is a common thread that runs through most of the mountains of studies on tobacco use.

Some also believe that increasing taxes will force the poor into quitting by making smoking unaffordable; however, the situation in New York City has shown that is not the case. *The American Journal of Public Health* did a detailed report in August 2007 of what happened in that city.

Back in 2002 cigarette taxes were increased by sixteen states, including New York. New York City also boosted its city excise tax from eight cents a pack to a whopping $1.50 a pack, putting the average cost of a package of cigarettes at $7.50 to $8 in New York City.

The result was a remarkable 11 percent drop in overall smoking rates. Then, however, the city reported an increase in smuggling and an increase in blatant street sales of contraband cigarettes. Contraband activity was especially noticeable in low-income neighbourhoods where traditional popular brands could be bought for $5 a pack.

Through surveys, the city estimated an 89 percent increase in cigarettes purchased through alternative channels, such as street vendors, the Internet, and other sources outside the city and the state.

Street vendors were everywhere, as many as twenty to a block, selling black-market cigarettes for $5 a pack, including in hospitals. They walked the streets with bags of cigarettes slung over their shoulders shouting "cigarettes, $5." People began calling the street vendors "the $5 man."

Smokers and non-smokers alike came to view the $5 man as justifiable in poor neighbourhoods. Said one: "We're thankful for the $5 man. Everyone is happy that the fare is gonna go back down. We're happy that we found the man on 125th Street that says Newport $5. We don't care that the cops are standing right there and he's doin' something illegal. It's not very important down on 86th Street, Central Park West."

Many people came to see the $5 man as a benefit to the community. The $5 men were creating economic benefit for themselves while providing a little financial relief to low-income smokers. For the poor, smoking provides relief from the stress of unemployment, poverty, lower education, and substandard living conditions.

The New York study concluded that even though interest in quitting smoking was high, the $5-man phenomenon created an environment in which it was easier to access cheap cigarettes than it was to access government programs to help people quit. In poor areas few people were aware of the cessation help available to them.

Not only is smoking more prevalent among the poor, it is harder for them to quit successfully. In 2012 City College of New York reported research showing that people with the fewest social and financial resources are two and one-half times more likely to resume smoking after six months of treatment than more affluent smokers. It said the poor have more stress and life's difficulties drive them back to cigarettes. Also, the poor live and work among more smokers, increasing the temptation to resume smoking.

A 2009 Gallup poll showed that 34 percent of American smokers earned less than $12,000 a year, compared with only 13 percent of those earning $90,000 or more. More than one-half — 53 percent — of smokers earned less than $36,000.

The smoking rate for American adults living above the poverty line is 20.6 percent, compared with 29.1 percent for those living in poverty. The poverty line at the start of 2012 was roughly $22,300 a year for a family of four. So, tobacco is a gauge for measuring the stresses of the poor.

New York revealed the heavy burden on the poor who can't quit the addiction when taxes increase. They are individual victims in the broad sweep to eliminate smoking in the interests of collective better health.

This is a developing issue for low-income families, where tobacco is a significant part of family expenses, especially in developing countries. In Bulgaria low-income households with at least one smoker spent 10.4 percent of total income on cigarettes. Urban households in Tibet spent 5.5 percent of household income on tobacco, while some households in China spent 17 percent of household income on smoking. The figures are old, from the 1990s, but illustrate the potential for problems as more pressure is applied to reduce smoking rates through tax increases.

It also can be an issue closer to home. In Canada, a husband and wife each smoking roughly one carton of fully taxed cigarettes a week would spend approximately $5,000 a year. If they both worked low-income jobs earning $25,000 a year, smoking would consume 10 percent of their annual household income.

Tobacco tax increases do help to reduce smoking rates. They do more good than harm, but the folks who put them in place must pay more attention to options that minimize the hardships for those who continue to smoke.

Parts of the New York City experience are easily related to First Nations reserves in Canada. Fifty percent of Native children on- and off-reserve live in poverty, the Royal Commission on Aboriginal Peoples reported in 1996. Presumably, their parents do as well, meaning that one-half of Canada's Native people live below the poverty line.

It should be no surprise then, notes the British Columbia Centre of Excellence for Women's Health, that, "given the marginalized and oppressive conditions facing many Aboriginal people and communities," smoking rates are much higher in Native communities.

Roughly 60 percent of people on First Nations reserves smoke. More than half of those started smoking between ages thirteen and sixteen. At least 60 percent of Native women smoke during pregnancy, compared with 26 percent of non-Native women.

The B.C. centre also adds: "It is important to note that, as in the non-Aboriginal population, smoking is much less common among Aboriginal people who are employed, who have higher incomes, and who have a university education."

Native companies make cigarettes that are sold to their people tax free, providing them jobs and other economic benefits, but at the same time making it harder for the addicted to quit. In Ontario there are reserve quotas, but in some places the quotas are as high as one thousand cartons per year per smoker. That's two hundred thousand cigarettes a year, or more than five hundred cigarettes a day!

The situation in New York City is similar to that in the Native communities in that they each have community members helping other members economically with cheaper tobacco, but at the same time making it easier for them to continue an unhealthy habit.

All this illustrates the intense complexity of contraband cigarette issues.

19

We're Not Alone

Our focus is often so fixed on troubled places like Akwesasne that we forget that we are not alone with contraband cigarette problems, or the quest to find solutions. Cigarette smuggling is a huge and profitable business loaded with complex problems in almost every country in the world. There is no national border in the world that has not been breached by illicit tobacco.

Worldwide, no legal consumer product is smuggled more than the cigarette. The World Health Organization, citing various government reports, says that in one year 846 billion cigarettes were exported around the world but only 619 billion were officially imported. That's a difference of 227 billion cigarettes that vanished into the contraband market. Add to that the counterfeit cigarettes and other cigarettes illicitly manufactured specifically for the black market and you have a huge illegal market.

Various studies put the size of the worldwide contraband cigarette market at between 6 and 10 percent, or more, of the legal market. The International Union Against Tuberculosis and Lung disease has estimated contraband at 12 percent, costing governments €35 billion a year in lost tax revenues.

World production is 5.7 trillion cigarettes a year. So, the number of black-market cigarettes is mind boggling, somewhere around three to five hundred billion a year, a number that makes

Canada's 2008 total seizures of two hundred million cigarettes look rather insignificant. The point is that we are not alone with the contraband problem and much of the world is working on solutions.

An example of this work is the Framework Convention on Tobacco Control (FCTC), which is a legally binding global treaty committing its signatories to achieve prescribed targets in tobacco control. This includes control programs such as taxation, advertising bans, warning labels, stop-smoking programs, and the creation of smoke-free environments. As of May 2011, the convention had 173 signatories, covering 87 percent of the world's population.

For Canadians, the country's black-market cigarette problems often seem larger and more dramatic than they really are, especially when compared with those of the United States. In fact, the United States has serious contraband tobacco issues, ones that are as large and complicated as Canada's.

The American smoking rate is about the same as Canada. The U.S. Centers for Disease Control and Prevention reports that in 2010 there were 45.3 million Americans, or 19.3 percent of the population, who smoked cigarettes. Substantial as this number is, it represents a significant decline from the statistics for 1965, the peak year for smoking in the United States, when 52 percent of American men and 32 percent of women smoked.

Tobacco smuggling has remained a serious U.S. problem, even as smoking rates declined. In fact, smuggling has grown in the past few years as more than one-half of states increased tobacco taxes. In 2010 the U.S. Department of Justice prosecuted seventy-one new tobacco smuggling cases, a 39-percent increase from 2009. The Bureau of Alcohol, Tobacco, Firearms and Explosives had 350 open cases in 2010, compared with only a handful ten years before.

Americans spend close to $90 billion a year on cigarettes, and the U.S. government estimates that federal and state governments lose about $5 billion in taxes to smuggling.

For some time, however, stories about cigarette smuggling in the United States were just not in the news as much. That's because after 9/11 the United States riveted its focus on terrorism. Van loads of illicit cigarettes were far down on the list of concerns for law-enforcement agencies that were spending their days and nights trying to prevent some terrorist maniac from slipping into the country with an atomic bomb.

Contraband cigarettes are receiving more U.S. attention now, however, because law-enforcement agencies have uncovered links between the illicit tobacco trade and terrorist groups. The unsettling "Lackawanna Seven" terrorism case, for example, had smuggled cigarette connections.

The case involved seven young men who grew up in Lackawanna, New York, outside Buffalo. They lived in a tight-knit Arab community, but were regular American teenagers who played soccer and went to parties. In the summer of 2001, the seven travelled to Afghanistan, where the U.S. government said they attended an Al-Qaeda terrorist training camp. Six returned to the United States; when questioned about where they had travelled, four said they had attended religious seminars in Pakistan. The FBI investigated, and further interrogated the men. Eventually, all six pleaded guilty to aiding a terrorist organization. They received sentences ranging from seven to ten years in prison. The seventh is believed to have gone to Yemen, and the United States has put a $5 million reward on his capture.

The seven got money to travel to Afghanistan from a man who was convicted in 2004 of money laundering and cigarette smuggling.

In another case, a crime group smuggled cigarettes from North Carolina, where the tax was $0.50 a carton, to Michigan, where the tax was $7.50 a carton. Prosecutors alleged that the group made $8 million profit in four years and that $100,000 of that was sent to the terrorist group Hezbollah.

The Bureau of Alcohol, Tobacco and Firearms and Explosives (ATF) has been using sting operations to get inside crime organizations that use illicit cigarette money to fund terrorism. In fact, in 2010 it was learned that ATF had directed 250 million cigarettes onto U.S. streets as part of its efforts to become involved with smugglers. These cigarettes became part of the black market and some ended up in the pockets and purses of young people. The ATF even opened a wholesale cigarette store in Virginia, which advertised in Arabic language newspapers. The sting saw sixty million cigarettes sold and twenty-seven people arrested.

There has been criticism that such stings put more contraband cigarettes on the streets. Others have criticized these operations for targeting minorities, saying that they involve racial profiling since the ads are placed in newspapers aimed at specific groups, such as Arabs. Another criticism is that such operations are merely a funding scheme for the agencies, since the law-enforcement agencies know that tying terrorism to any anti-crime initiative is a way to attract attention and get more support, financial and otherwise.

ATF agents counter these criticisms by claiming that even though tobacco stings might not produce enough evidence to lay terrorism charges, they do disrupt terrorism financing, and that they have jailed people involved in terrorism.

Much of the cigarette smuggling in the United States involves diversion from low-tax states to high-tax states. The federal cigarette tax is standard at just over $1 a pack. State taxes vary from $0.17 a pack in Missouri to $4.35 in New York State. The average state excise tax was $1.46 a pack in 2012. Some cities, like New York City, also apply a municipal tax.

The profits available to smugglers who illegally move cigarettes from one state to another are significant. For example, if an organized crime ring spent $2.03 million to fill a tractor-trailer with cigarettes bought for $4.29 a pack, taxes included, at retail outlets in Missouri, drove the truckload to New York City and sold them on the streets for $5 a pack, their profit would be roughly $330,000 for that one load. If an individual did the same thing, throwing three cases of cigarettes into the back of a van and driving to New York to sell them on the streets, his profit would be roughly $1,000 for just three boxes.

As a result of its lucrativeness, smuggling across state borders is rampant and impossible to stop completely. How do you stop someone from driving a couple miles across a nearly invisible state line to buy two cartons of cigarettes for personal use at a savings of $10 a carton? Law-enforcement agencies know that they can't do anything substantial about this casual smuggling so they focus instead on "commercial" smuggling, i.e., organized smuggling of large quantities of cigarettes between states.

U.S. authorities have also been busy finding ways to stop the astounding growth of Internet cigarette sales that avoid taxation. Research has shown that the number of Internet cigarette vendors has grown significantly in recent years, from fewer than one hundred ten years ago to about eight hundred today. Roughly one-half of those vendors operate outside North America, some selling counterfeit brands. Internet vendors within the United States include Indian operations, and others working from low-tax states such as Kentucky, North Carolina, and Virginia.

Internet sales are profitable because the vendors do not collect federal, state, or provincial taxes. Vendors outside North America say they are exempt from collecting taxes because they operate outside the country. Natives say they are exempt because they have sovereign status.

Much effort has been directed into stopping Internet sales, which create two major problems for governments: they create tax losses and they allow access for young smokers who are seeing more and more restrictions at the traditional retail level.

Major credit card companies and major private shippers in the United States agreed in 2005 to refuse transactions involving cigarettes sold over the Internet. In 2010 a new U.S. federal law, the Prevent All Cigarette Trafficking (PACT) Act, took effect, making cigarettes a non-mailable item and requiring all Internet cigarette vendors to verify the age and identity of customers and to pay all applicable taxes.

These actions have cut deeply into Internet sales; however, cigarette buyers can still pay by cheque, money order, or even cash. Shipments can be disguised. Where there is a will, there is a way.

As in Canada, a growing source of discount cigarettes in the United States has been Native reserves. Some U.S. tribes sell huge numbers of popular, brand-name cigarettes, as well as their own brands, without taxes. U.S. courts have generally ruled that cigarettes sold on tribal lands to Native Americans are exempt from state excise taxes unless authorized by federal law. Sales to non-Indians, on the other hand, are generally held to be taxable.

Some tribes have accepted that and have entered into agreements with the government to collect taxes on cigarettes sold on reserves. An example: in the 1990s, Jerry Montour, one of the founders of Grand River Enterprises near Brantford, Ontario, helped a Nebraska tribe establish the Omaha Nation Tobacco Company. The company had an ATF licence and Montour said in a National Public Radio interview at the time that the company paid all federal and state taxes and intended to compete with other cigarette companies by undercutting their prices.

In some cases the taxes are used by tribal governments for health, education, and other reserve needs.

In the past few years, Native taxation agreements have been worked out between Canadian governments and a small number of Native communities.

The largest Native vendor of tax-free cigarettes in the United States has been the Seneca Nation in New York, which has had close ties to other Iroquois nation tribes, including Mohawks on the Canadian side of the border.

New York State has tried vigorously to stop the tribes from selling untaxed cigarettes to non-Natives. In 2011 it won a major court victory that affirmed its right to collect taxes on cigarette sales on Native land, and immediately began a crackdown. In response, the Senecas, and other related tribes, stopped bringing in national brands for resale, deciding to sell only their own manufactured cigarettes. The Senecas now have four licensed manufacturing plants on their lands and others are considering opening their own.

This development will likely result in the Indians losing some revenue and the state gaining some, since brand-loyal smokers can no longer buy their Marlboros, Camels, and Winstons at reservation stores. However, the Indians hope smokers will forgo brand loyalty in favour of large savings offered by Native brands. They say that if the state tries to force tax collection on Native brands, the years of court battling will resume.

Beyond North America's shores, the statistics relating to smoking and contraband issues are stunning. One-seventh, or just under one billion, of the world's seven billion people smoke. Their numbers will increase despite the relentless pursuit of the tobacco-control industry. That's because the world population is expected to increase by two billion by the year 2030. Even if smoking rates fall, the number of cigarette consumers might remain the same simply because of the population growth.

While tobacco growing has declined steadily in North America since the 1964 Surgeon General's Report linking smoking and cancer, it has increased in Africa and Asia, and it is now grown in 125-plus countries. It has almost doubled in China, Malawi, and Tanzania.

North America still rates high in the total number of cigarettes consumed at 745 billion. It is followed by Eastern Europe and former Soviet economies (631 billion) and Western Europe (606 billion). Asia, Australia, and the Far East are by far the largest consumers (2,715 billion cigarettes).

Smuggling rates vary from region to region (and rates for individual regions vary depending on who does the estimating). The highest estimated smuggling rate is 10.7 percent of world production, provided by the World Health Organization. Its percentage estimate works out to six hundred billion illicit cigarettes a year.

Deutsche Zigarettenverband, the German Cigarette Association, said that in 2011 more than 22 percent of the cigarettes smoked in Germany had not been taxed. The number of untaxed cigarettes smoked was estimated at 23.5 billion or 1.5 billion more than 2010. Revenue lost to the German government was estimated at €5.5 billion.

European Union studies put Europe cigarette smuggling at 8.5 percent of production.

Whatever the numbers, one conclusion is obvious: Smoking is not going to go away for a long, long time, if ever. North America and some other parts of the world have made impressive progress in the fight against smoking, but less impressive is the progress against contraband.

Photo: Courtesy World Health Organization

As tobacco growing has declined steadily in North America, it has increased in Africa and Asia. It has almost doubled in China, Malawi, and Tanzania. So has production of tobacco leaves — to seven million metric tonnes between 1960 and 2000. Child labour, as seen with this Thai boy, is still used in tobacco production in some parts of the world.

Not only has the amount of contraband trade in cigarettes increased, so too has the variety of criminal types involved in the illicit tobacco trade. They now include single, extemporary criminals, professional traders, Mafia-type groups, and also terrorist organizations. Criminal activity in contraband cigarettes has expanded from quick and clever smuggling schemes to make occasional money, to a well-planned, well-directed industry.

Along with the sale of contraband cigarettes, the counterfeiting of brand-name cigarettes, plus the production of "cheap whites" — cigarettes made specifically for the black market — have become a growing part of the illicit industry. Taken together, they represent a flood of illegal product, which the police find almost impossible to stop.

Of course, the greatest impediment to solving the contraband cigarette problem is one that is constant throughout the world: the large number of willing consumers. While cigarette-tax evasion has become somewhat stigmatized in Canada and the United States, there are many parts of the world where it is not considered a serious problem.

A document prepared for a 2011 European Union round table notes the public lack of knowledge about the consequences of contraband tobacco: "... the stigma normally associated with much criminal activity does not always apply to the Illicit Trade in Tobacco Products (ITTP). This is because the population frequently does not have full knowledge of the seriousness and consequences of the ITTP and also because tobacco products, contrary to e.g. illicit drugs and firearms, are still considered an everyday commodity, easily accessible to most adults citizens."

In today's hectic societies, people are so time-starved and so swamped with information that they seldom spend the time required to develop a thorough understanding of the critical issues facing them. However, it is only by people educating themselves about the costs of smuggling and the effects of their participation in smuggling operations that this problem can ever be eradicated. Police surveillance, roadblocks, and raids can never eliminate contraband tobacco. A public informed about smuggling and its consequences can.

20

Stereotyping

The increasing Native involvement in the tobacco industry is bad news and good news. Tobacco is not a preferred pathway into economic development, but it has created jobs and brought money into Native communities, notably Six Nations, Kahnawake, and other reserves in Quebec and reservations in New York State. Hopefully, the jobs and money will be a base for building other enterprises.

The bad news should be obvious: tobacco use sickens and kills. And when cigarettes become contraband, they bring criminal activity and pick the pockets of government. Citizens are the people who fill those pockets, so when they are picked, each of us loses money. Tobacco is a legal product, however, and people, Natives and others, have a right to grow it, and to manufacture and sell tobacco products provided that they follow the rules and restrictions placed upon them.

The really bad news is that the increasing role of Natives in the tobacco trade has not done anything to eliminate the stereotyping of Native people. If anything, it has increased stereotyping, with non-Natives now viewing Natives as either as part of illicit tobacco activity, or as legitimate business people selling disease and death.

Columbus saw the Indians as naked and wild innocents — morally inferior beings that were to be Christianized, civilized, and exploited. His view put the first brush strokes on the Indian image. Increased contact and conflicts added other qualities — savage, stealthy, treacherous, warlike — to the image. Then the individual stereotypes took shape: the Indian princess, the wise and toothless elder, the drunk sleeping in the back alley, the dedicated environmentalist, and the angry and dangerous young radical.

From land rights confrontations and warrior societies emerged the image of the Native in combat camo clothing and bandanas. The trade in discount cigarettes, whether illicit or legally manufactured and sold, created the image of the Native person as a smuggler.

Politicians and police sometimes use these stereotypes to help justify their actions. For instance, although the Oka crisis began as a Mohawk defensive action, the warriors were labelled as criminals and terrorists, and their actions were portrayed as offensive, something that must be stopped.

In fact, Oka began because Mohawks objected to the building of a golf course on land they considered sacred, and which they felt belonged to them. Bull-headed politicians and others followed the old colonial thinking: push impediments such as the Indians out of the way, and get on with building something important.

Such simplistic and colonial-era thinking is common too in discussions of Natives and tobacco. However, the issues of contraband cigarette and of Native involvement in the cigarette industry are not cut and dried like tobacco. Some Natives no doubt are involved in the contraband cigarette trade, as are many other people of different nationalities and races. There are also other Natives manufacturing and distributing legal cigarettes. They are allowed to sell cigarettes free or partially free of taxes, depending on the jurisdiction, but too often their activities get lumped in with the illegal activities of others.

Native sovereignty is an important factor in the issues. Some Native groups say they have the right to manufacture cigarettes on their own territory, without authorization from outside governments. This is, for them, all part of the struggle to regain the self-determination lost over decades of non-Native rule.

Stereotypes are images fixed in our minds, often defying logic and lacking real evidence. They become imbedded and are difficult to remove. The fact that Native stereotypes continue to exist in our rigidly politically correct society is disturbing. The kind of Native stereotyping that we allow to exist would not be tolerated if applied to other races.

Native stereotyping grew from that colonial dream of clearing the land of all obstacles to settlement. It was assumed that assimilation or extinction would make the Indian problem go away. When the Indians did not go away or assimilate, the settler population began to see Natives as a lesser people stubbornly stuck in the past, incapable of advancing like the rest of the country.

The news media bears much of the responsibility for perpetuating stereotyping of Native groups. Newspapers especially helped to shape, maintain, and reshape images of Natives that are based on colonial thinking. The power and influence of newspapers is in steep decline, but for more than a century they reflected the views of those in authority — politicians, major business institutions, and law enforcement. Those groups focused on the impediments and problems in Natives communities, which would not or could not fit into the bigger society., Focusing on the impediments and problems that existed, the news media seldom reported on matters that would help develop understanding of Native life.

Even when trying to understand and help Native populations, the media unconsciously perpetuate Native stereotypes. News reporting leaves little time or space for background, perspective, or context. Routine reporting of Native living conditions, although often meant to highlight conditions that need fixing, add to the stereotyping.

There are roughly 1.2 million Aboriginal people in Canada. Statistics Canada data from 2006 shows that 45 percent of people on reserves live in dwellings needing major repair. Only 7 percent of people on reserves had a university degree compared with 25 percent of non-Native Canadians. Forty percent had less than a high school education compared with 13 percent for the rest of the population. Native life expectancies are lower and so are employment levels.

The statistics and constant reporting of conditions of misery reinforce an image of Natives as being inferior. The implication is that if they are behind the rest of us in so many categories, they must be incapable or unwilling to help themselves. They receive billions of dollars in assistance from governments but seem to keep falling behind. So, it must be their fault.

Such statements defy logic. Native people have done remarkable things, during pre-European days and since the Native revival of the 1960s. Their ancient inventions such as the canoe, the kayak, the toboggan, and snowshoes are examples of brilliant design, and they have proved their worth, with few changes beyond materials, over the centuries. Now Natives are showing industry and innovation in an advanced overall society. They are constitutional scholars, pilots, engineers, doctors, lawyers, teachers, and business leaders. Many have progressed into the world of the larger society while maintaining, and even strengthening, traditional beliefs and practices. Others continue to maintain the Native approach to living, maintaining unique thought processes, languages, and traditions that far pre-date non-Native arrival in North America.

The stories of Native people's successes, in their communities or as part of the larger society, are not told often enough, or from the Native viewpoint. If they do get told, they often are lost in news coverage of desperate conditions in places like Attawapiskat, Ontario, or in confrontations like Oka.

When reporting on Native affairs, the media tends to give prominence to the elected leadership of Native communities. Warrior factions, traditionalists, groups that do not have official authority are reported as "self-proclaimed," the implication being that they have no status among the "legitimate" voices of the people. This is often done with little context or understanding of the complex history of Native governance.

News reporting remains based on the colonial idea that we need to eliminate the "Indian problem" to get on with developing the country. Canada and the United States approached "the Indian problem" in different ways, but the outcomes have been much the same.

The United States followed its military nose, fighting the Indians, rounding them up and marching them onto reservations where they would be out of the way. Its approach to the problem was to remove it. The resulting trails of tears, so the official line goes, were regretful but necessary, and could be romanticized later, with a few pretty Indian princesses and wise toothless elders tossed in to soften the story.

Canada followed a policy of assimilation and thought itself much more humane and understanding because of it. It negotiated treaties, many of which were altered or broken later, and set itself up as the protector and benefactor of Native peoples. It saw its approach as much superior to the United States

Neither approach made "the Indian problem" go away, however. Neither did residential schools, designed to strip Native children of their language and culture. Nor did the Trudeau government's attempts at the elimination of special status for Natives by means of its 1969 white paper, which proposed to abolish the Indian Act, and reject the land claims and the distinctness of Native people.

The white paper proposed making Natives the same as any other ethnic minority. Stiff opposition from Native people and later Supreme Court of Canada decisions on land rights forced the government to abandon the approach. Instead of eliminating Natives as a distinct people, the white paper fired up opposition that helped to build the modern Canadian Native rights movement.

Most of our knowledge of Native people comes from the media, and much of the news reporting focuses either on conflicts or poor living conditions, both topics that support the colonial view that Native people are troublesome and lacking the qualities that made the European peoples nation builders. There have been few opportunities to alter this view because most in mainstream society have only intermittent contact with Native society. Natives live in separate communities, or in ghettos in urban centres. Non-Natives have some romantic notions about some of their traditions, but for most people, the overall knowledge and understanding of Native people's journey under colonial domination is shallow.

While the media help to create and sustain Native stereotypes, it also gets trapped by them and lured into biased coverage. York University researchers Dr. Frances Henry and Carol Tator studied media coverage of the trials of Jack Ramsay, a member of Parliament tried in 1999–2000 for attempted rape of a fourteen-year-old Native girl thirty years earlier. Ramsay was an RCMP officer at the time of the alleged crime.

The York researchers found that the media portrayed Ramsay as a Native rights advocate and a family man, someone with strong principles and a history of service. The girl was portrayed as coming from alcoholic parents, someone from a troubled community with alcohol and drug problems of her own.

Ramsay was convicted of attempted rape and sentenced to nine months in jail. The conviction was overturned on appeal. At a second trial, Ramsay pleaded guilty to a lesser charge of indecent assault and was sentenced to probation and community service.

Media coverage of Native matters is not likely to improve or deepen in the future unless people make dedicated attempts to become more knowledgeable. Today's media, even if it became more thorough and balanced in Native affairs coverage, is unlikely to help. The decline of newspapers and battered news budgets throughout the media have left huge black holes on the news coverage map of North America. Much of Native living occurs in these black holes and we hear less and less of what goes on there, unless it is sensational. It is, therefore, confrontation, violence, or something else that connects Native people and trouble that usually makes the news.

We now have an unfocused media feeding a society too busy to pay much attention. Much of the "news" coverage found on television today consists merely of pieces of entertainment or of politicians standing before cameras spouting the party line. This coverage is easier and less expensive to produce than thoughtful and detailed reporting. There is, however, a huge amount of knowledge on the Internet to allow anyone to build themselves a thorough and balanced view of what is happening in Native affairs today. That requires interest, and of course plenty of time.

In the meantime, stereotyping continues to evolve. The violent warrior, once subdued, became the indolent welfare case. The 1960s revival brought back the warrior image. Emerging now is an image of corruption and incompetence developed from stories about poor management of band affairs.

Political and business interests have good reason to promote this stereotype. Native peoples are exerting more pressure and gaining support in their efforts to regain land and its resources. The many interests promoting pipelines and hydro-electric developments and other colossal projects see the Native pressure as a serious threat.

They have an interest in pointing out cases of Native mismanagement. However, excellent guidance, education, and experiences are beginning to produce more cases of Native successes.

Native societies must find ways of using traditional values and approaches to creating a distinct society within our larger society. That is a difficult, if not impossible task, unless stereotyping of Native people is eliminated. Our society must see and accept Native people for what they are: a distinct culture working against a miserable past to build a valued society within a much larger society.

The Royal Commission on Aboriginal Peoples said in 1996: "Violence in Aboriginal communities is promoted and sustained by racist attitudes that perpetuate demeaning stereotypes, especially of Aboriginal women.

"The living, changing cultures of Aboriginal peoples have an important role in helping to overturn the myths and stereotypes, twisted facts and misunderstandings that prevail in much of non-Aboriginal Canada. Doing so will require dialogue with knowledgeable Aboriginal communicators."

York researchers Henry and Tator have been more direct in their views:

> Racial profiling is not simply the sum of individual actions of "a few bad apples." Nor is it exclusively the product of dominant White values, beliefs, and norms as they are reflected in police culture. Nor is it simply the result of outmoded, hierarchical, and militaristic approaches to the policing of crime. Rather, racial profiling is an aggregate of all of these elements. It is a reflection of the racism that links all institutional spaces. This web of institutions includes legislatures and bureaucracies, the criminal justice system, the media, schools and universities, and the vehicles of popular culture. All

of these in concert reinforce racism in the mainstream
White culture as well as in police culture.

Examples of how Natives are stereotyped are not difficult to
find, despite authoritative calls against them. Because Mohawks
have a history as steelworkers, stories spread in the 1990s of how
easily they could use their steel-working skills to blow up bridges.

Too often people who should know better are reckless in the
words they about Natives.

Robert Bourassa, Quebec premier during the Oka crisis, said
it was difficult to defend democracy against people who do not
believe in democracy. That was directed at the Mohawks, who
were protesting what they saw as a lack of democracy in government dealings with them.

Brian Mulroney, when he was prime minister, said his government would not accede to the request of warriors, some of
whom were not Canadian citizens and who were involved in illegal
activities. That was a broad attack and insulted Mohawks whose
Akwesasne territory is neither Canadian nor American.

The Canadian Armed Forces, in a 2006 draft manual, called
the Mohawk Warrior Society an example of the "radical Native
American organizations" that can be "viewed as insurgencies with
specific and limited aims." It was mentioned along with Hezbollah
and the Taliban, both considered terrorists organizations.

In 2008 Dick Pound, McGill University Chancellor and Canadian International Olympic Committee representative, said that four
hundred years ago Canada was a land inhabited by "savages." That
brought protests from Native communities and Pound said it was a
clumsy comment made in French. The phrase "pays de sauvages" did
not have the same meaning as "savages" in English, he said.

Through centuries of stereotyping, intended or just careless
slips, Native people have shown a remarkable resilience. Despite

being characterized as lesser beings or less capable people, they have clung doggedly to the traditions and beliefs that have sustained them as a distinct and strong culture determined to survive.

The Royal Commission on Aboriginal Peoples commented on this survival instinct: "Assimilation policies failed because Aboriginal people have the secret of cultural survival. They have an enduring sense of themselves as peoples with a unique heritage and the right to cultural continuity.

"This is what drives them when they blockade roads, protest at military bases and occupy scared grounds. This is why they resist pressure to merge into Euro-Canadian society — a form of cultural suicide urged upon them in the name of 'equality' and 'modernization.'"

We all must start getting to know and understand Native people much better. That sounds ridiculous after five hundred years of living together, but basically what we know of Native people, we get from the media. Gerald Taiaiake Alfred has summed it up: "The Canadian population itself, as distinct from authorities, has little direct experience with indigenous peoples, and certainly not with the experience of indigenous resistances against the injustice of their situations as colonized peoples. Canadian society's understanding of indigenous resistance and warrior societies is largely framed by the mass media. Thus there is very little basis for an informed and critical engagement on the part of the population with the instrumental characterizations developed by police and political authorities."

21

Dancing

Parliament Hill in Ottawa is the dance capital of Canada. There they know and practise all the steps, including the shuffle, the soft shoe, the shuck and jive, and the sly-as-a-fox trot.

In April 2010 the Hill witnessed an excellent performance of tap dancing around the contraband tobacco problem. It occurred at a meeting of the House of Commons Standing Committee on Public Safety and National Security. The committee heard from a variety of witnesses in yet another effort to find solutions to the cigarette problem that will not go away.

A Bloc Québécois member, Maria Mourani of Ahuntsic, Quebec, said in a preamble to a question to the RCMP that the majority of contraband comes from four or five reserves in Ontario and Quebec. She said there are about one hundred unlicensed and illegal cigarette factories feeding 80 to 90 percent of the illegal market.

Then she asked her question: "I would like to know, in concrete terms, why you don't close those plants down. Why are factories that do not have licences allowed to keep blithely operating? How is it that laws that are enforced everywhere in Canada by convenience stores and other stores are not enforced on reserves?"

The RCMP began dancing. There are probably only fifty illegal factories, not one hundred, they said…. Many illegal cigarettes come from the United States.... The RCMP prefers to target and disrupt organized crime groups, rather than specific facilities.

Ms. Mourani was unimpressed by that exhibition of shuffling and heel and toe taps.

"Unless I'm mistaken, tobacco factories have to have licences, both federal and provincial," she said. "If the plants don't have licences, they are illegal. How can the RCMP tell us not to take action against the factories? I have to admit I don't understand."

Police operations, said the RCMP, require that officer safety and public safety be considered also. The police find ways of achieving an objective without putting public at risk.

"What do you mean by the term 'public safety'?" asked Ms. Mourani. "What are you afraid of? That the Mohawks will decide to blockade a bridge, or a road? Is that what you mean by public safety?"

"Not speaking of any individuals, there are always considerations when police operations take place in areas that are politically sensitive," replied the RCMP.

Despite the dancing, the issue was there for everyone to see. Plainly put, police forces are terrified by the thought of raiding illegal tobacco factories on Native land. There have been calls for police action against the reserves, but no police commander in his or her right mind would order it. Nor would any politician.

Having law enforcement shut down illegal cigarette operations in Native communities would dry up a good chunk of the contraband supply. That should never happen, however, and not just for reasons of public or police safety. Enforcement on reserves almost certainly would bring violence. Many Natives would see the police presence as an invasion of sovereign land by a foreign power. An outside police presence would have to be constant, or at least regular, to stop the illegal factories from rebuilding.

Most importantly, strict enforcement of tobacco laws on Native territory would damage severely any efforts to solve tobacco problems, and the many issues accompanying them. The tobacco trade is part of a package of problems that must be worked out among Native people themselves, and between Native nations and Canada. Police raids to enforce tobacco laws would signal that, once again, force is the government's preferred method of dealing a problem with Native communities, rather than working together with the Natives on solutions, and helping displaced people find their place within the overall society.

So, as much as possible, the politicians and the police try to avoid the use of force in their efforts to confront the issue of contraband tobacco on reserves. Of course, this means that, strictly speaking, the police are often not upholding the law as it has been set forth by the politicians. This makes the role of the police — those charged with enforcing the law in Native tobacco issues — an unenviable one. Making the RCMP dance before a political committee makes their position even worse; it is a waste of time and an embarrassment to the officers involved. The issue of contraband tobacco in Native communities is a political problem, not a police problem, and it's unfair to ask the police to go before the politicians and dance around questions it is not their business to answer.

It's not that police never raid reserves where cigarettes are being manufactured illegally. They do, but they say they are after drugs, not tobacco. In the summer of 2011, for example, a large force of RCMP, SQ, and Native police raided Kanesatake to bust a drug ring also operating out of Kahnawake and Akwesasne.

Such raids are generally accepted on reserves, sometimes even requested, because the people don't want the drug trade and the criminal activities it brings to any community. Tobacco, legal or not, is another matter. Although some Natives do not accept the tobacco trade as proper, many see it as part of their fight for self-determination.

Meetings like the April 2010 gathering on Parliament Hill are simply political puppet shows. They provide a stage for martinets who wish to be seen as engaged in trying to solve a critical national issue. However, the politicians' jaw-flapping and dancing around are hardly suitable substitutes for top-drawer thinking, negotiations, and executive action. The military-style law enforcement that is usually called for by these figures as a way of solving the problem of the illegal tobacco trade is the last thing that is needed, especially given the costs involved.

Over the past several decades, law-enforcement costs related to contraband tobacco have increased steadily. However, the public will never know by how much because agencies like the RCMP and Canada Revenue Agency will never give a true exact cost of fighting contraband.

It is possible to speculate, however, based on some factual information. The number of RCMP personnel has increased 50 percent in the past twelve years, rising from twenty thousand to thirty thousand members. Headquarters staff in Ottawa doubled to 4,569 members during that period as did RCMP spending. Staff and resources assigned to contraband tobacco has increased regularly, especially with the much-publicized enforcement pushes in 2008 and 2010.

Rather than fighting it with increased policing, the contraband cigarette trade could be delivered a knockout blow by lowering tobacco taxes, as was done in 1994. This would shock and infuriate the large and powerful tobacco control industry, of course. That industry, which includes government agencies, various societies working against diseases, lobby groups, and others, has convincing evidence that higher taxes help to lower smoking rates, which in turn reduce health-care burdens and save lives.

Lowering taxes thins the profit incentive for black market operators. High profits are worth the risk of dealing in illegal products. When the profit is significantly reduced, why be involved? Black-market cigarette seizures were at their lowest levels in the twenty-plus years between 1990 and 2009 following the 1994 tax reductions.

There is no solid evidence that smoking rates increased dramatically because of the lower taxes. There is evidence that the lower prices offered by black marketeers not only do not help people to quit smoking, but they in fact make it easier for young people to start.

Little attention has been given to the increasing law-enforcement costs. If the public had accurate figures on law-enforcement costs, it would be able to better judge the most effective ways of fighting the contraband tobacco problem. To gauge the total cost, however, all costs must be taken into account. Costs include not only expenditures on police, equipment, and infrastructure; they also include the cost of more people handling more illegal cigarette cases in the justice system — something that costs us all a lot more.

Then there are the human costs too. Young people who are supposed to be readying themselves for productive lives are being lured into smuggling by greedy people who don't give a damn who gets hurt. The young, many of them underprivileged Natives enticed by quick money, become carriers, or mules, in the contraband system. The big-boy criminals know that a small percent of the mules will get caught, but the majority will slip through and make them money. For the bosses, the losses are just part of the game, and it doesn't matter to them if some of the kids who work for them are caught and end up in prison — the kids likely don't have much of a future anyway.

The violence associated with contraband tobacco, the disrespect for the law and government, the dissension among Native peoples, and the fostering of the attitude that something can be got for nothing all have costs for society. No one has done an inventory and stacked these costs beside the costs resulting from lower tax rates that would reduce black-market cigarettes.

This is not to advocate a cigarette tax cut like the one instituted by the panic-stricken Chrétien government in 1994. The arguments for the benefits of increasing tobacco taxes are clear and understood. What is not understood is whether the benefits outweigh the social costs of having a contraband problem encouraged by high taxation. This is a question that needs to be reviewed again seriously, free of the biases of the anti-tobacco campaigns.

Healthy skepticism and probing questions are necessary in today's environment. The tobacco control lobby has become obsessed with its mission of creating a smoke-free world. The world needs to thank these people for improving health and saving lives. However, it is time to ease up on the blizzard of scary statistics and hyperbole, take a few deep breaths, and carefully review where we are in the war against tobacco.

It is possibly true that high taxation is the most effective tactic against smoking. It cannot be given all the credit for reduced smoking rates, however. Prohibiting smoking in public places and work places, advertising and promotion bans, and sensible public education campaigns, have had major impacts. The question now is: are there other ways of cutting smoking rates that would also serve to eliminate the profit gaps that drive contraband?

Whatever decisions are made about the tobacco trade, one thing is certain: it will remain a central part of Native life. For the foreseeable future, it is likely that it will also remain an important part of the economic life of many Native communities in North America too. The Native commercial tobacco trade has grown into an important industry that helps to provide the needs of life in many Native communities. There are few places in North America where anyone can survive any more on the traditional work of hunting, fishing, and gathering. An alternative way of making a living has become necessary for most Natives. In the past twenty-five years, tobacco has increasingly provided work and revenue to impoverished Native communities.

However, tobacco will never provide a well-anchored footing for building strong economies in Native communities. Tobacco has few friends, and therefore tobacco revenue has a declining life expectancy. Despite the hand wringing in the tobacco control industry, and its overheated warnings and other displays of anxiety, smoking rates will continue to drop throughout the world. Even inside Native communities, where jobs and money are needed, there is some opposition to the development of a commercial tobacco industry, no matter how much money it might bring in. For the time being, though, the tobacco trade provides some much-needed income.

The real problem now is the same old problem that has been around for more than a century. How to find economies to replace the hunter-fisher-gatherer economy that supported Indian nations before colonialism, the breaking of the land, industrial development, growing populations, and pollution took it away? How to develop economies that fit Indian needs, cultures, traditions and aspirations?

So many factors work against Native economic development. A narrow focus on quick jobs can divert thinking and resources away from building a long-term economy. Leadership experience is sometimes lacking too, because non-Native governments have traditionally insisted on controlling too many aspects of Native life. Complicated Native politics, with its dissension between traditional and imposed band governments, can also hold back development. And, it must be admitted, some Natives simply do not want any economic development, preferring to live the way they always have.

Despite the negatives, some tribes in the United States and Canada have built flourishing economies that suit their needs and preferences. Researchers have been puzzled about why some tribes have done so well, while many others continue to suffer high unemployment, poverty, and substandard housing. Some of the success stories have been based on having natural resources, but others have been successful without having them.

The Harvard Project on American Indian Economic Development studied why some tribes have been successful and why others have not. It has suggested that Indian economic development must be created through nation building, not simply by trying to create jobs and money. Some of the project's thoughts have been pooh-poohed by researchers and bureaucrats in Canada who claimed that their findings were not applicable in this country, but that is often the case with American ideas that travel north. Any thinking on how to improve Native conditions should be embraced and examined sideways and upside down to determine if even scraps of it can be used to make improvements.

The Harvard Project suggests that tribes must effectively exercise their sovereignty to build viable nations in which both businesses and people can flourish, and an environment in which people want to invest. "Without sovereignty and nation-building," the Harvard Project has said, "economic development is likely to remain a frustratingly elusive dream."

With Native sovereignty — the people's right to self-determination, their right to make and live by their own rules — the Project sees an approach in which sustained community well-being is created through long-term economic planning strategies, and not just short-term jobs aimed at getting money into the community quickly. It also emphasizes the importance of measuring success through social, cultural, political, and economic impacts, rather than just by the economic impact.

The solutions to Native economic development are found not just in money, but, rather, in leadership, a sound tribal foundation, strategic direction, and informed action.

The Osoyoos band in British Columbia's Okanagan Valley provides an example of how Native communities can be successful. The band started achieving economic success by promoting its culture and traditions. The Nk'Mip Desert and Heritage Interpretive Centre has become a family tourism destination, offering an interpretive centre, indoor and outdoor exhibit galleries, plus activities such as rappelling and fishing.

It has other successful businesses, including Nk'Mip Cellars, a joint venture with Vincor International, North America's fourth-largest producer and marketer of wines.

Those successes have attracted attention and created confidence in the Osoyoos band's ability to run a business. Early in 2012 the B.C. government announced that a 360-cell prison would be built on Osoyoos band land. The band had invested $9 million of its money to create an industrial park to attract the prison and other businesses. The prison will provide jobs, long-term tax revenue, and a chance for Natives to help other Natives, who make up a disproportionate part of the B.C. prison population.

Unemployment on the reserve, once about 30 percent, is in the 9 percent range now. Government payments to the tribe, once the chief source of band funds, now make up only 10 percent of the band's annual budget.

On the other side of Canada, the Membertou Mi'kmaq First Nation in Nova Scotia has gone from total government dependence to near self-sufficiency in the past fifteen years. It created a corporate division that operates businesses ranging from an insurance company to a food service operation, a hotel, and a data centre.

The Conference Board of Canada has said that while successful Native communities encourage private businesses, band-owned enterprises are better. "Band-owned business enterprises are given priority because their focus is on community well-being rather than private profit. Also, the distribution of benefits and costs from their operations are better aligned with the Aboriginal values of sharing and respect for the environment."

Some Native tobacco operations have band involvement, but the majority are privately operated. Their overall contribution to the community, whether they are licensed or not, is that they bring money into the community. Grand River Enterprises gives back through its Dreamcatcher Fund, which provides grants for sports and other recreation, arts and culture, education, and health. The Kahnawake Tobacco Association has estimated that the tobacco industry on that reserve gives work to 1,700 to 2,000 people.

Centuries of stereotyping led to the belief that Natives cannot do well in business. That stereotype is being proved a lie by the growing number of Native business successes throughout North America. Natives, who were supposed to become extinct or assimilated, haven't disappeared. They are still around, and some of their nations are growing and developing, although others are still shocking examples of misery.

The fact that Natives have survived centuries of colonialism, numerous attempts at extinction and assimilation through things like residential schools, and enforced foreign governance is remarkable. It reveals an outstanding resiliency, and provides hope for the future.

Huge and ugly problems remain. They must be sorted out by Natives themselves, with guidance and coaching from the rest of us, not rules and bureaucratic approaches laid down by governments.

There is a Native legend that speaks to solving problems. You can witness the legend live at ceremonies in which the Hoop Dance is performed.

One version of the legend says that after the Great Turtle rose and marked the beginning of the world, an earth woman and the spirit Epingishmook had a son called Papeekawis, or Pukawiss or Babiikawis, depending on your tribe. He was the brother of Nanabush, the powerful joker, and Chibiabos who gave the Anishnabek the pipe. Papeekawis was the less known son, an entertainer would gave the people the Hoop Dance. Papeekawis intended the dance to show troubled people how to help themselves.

The dance begins when the dancer, male or female, enters the dance circle to an accompanying slow drumbeat. He or she carries a handful of willow hoops about one metre in diameter. The drumbeat accelerates and the dancer whirls and stabs the ground with his feet while encircling himself in the hoops, which represent life's troubles. The hoops spin on the dancer's arms and legs and torso trying to pull him down and overcome him. From the crowd, someone tosses another hoop, which the dancer catches and adds to the spinning collection. Then another. The troubles keep multiplying.

The dancer manipulates the hoops to form figures representing manitous like the snake, thunderbird, or eagle. The drumbeats quicken and the dancer dances furiously, changing the hoop figures as he calls on various manitous to help him out of his troubles. No matter how fast he or she dances, no matter how well the hoop figures are manipulated to plead with the manitous, there is no help.

Nearly exhausted, the hoop dancer realizes the only escape from the problems — the only way to become free — is to dance his or her way out of the hoops. One by one the hoops come off the arms and legs and neck as he dances, until suddenly he is free and all the hoops are in his hands. He or she has freed himself without help and has learned the great lesson of Papeekawis: to overcome life's problems you must confront them, and defeat them on your own.

Native nations must dance their way out of their own hoops. Non-Natives must stop tossing them new hoops, and provide understanding and encouragement in finding Native solutions in the Native way.

22

The Situation Today

A lmost one-quarter of a century has passed since the world saw that iconic photograph of Mohawk Warrior Brad Laroque and Canadian soldier Patrick Cloutier in a nose-to-nose standoff at Oka, Quebec. Throughout those years, the photo has become more than an image of the Oka trouble. It has become a symbol of the standoff between Canada and its Native peoples over tobacco and other issues.

The tobacco issue is larger and more complicated now. Disagreements continue over what tobacco is legal and what is illegal, with much of the disagreements tangled in arguments about sovereignty. Governments have gone after clearly defined tobacco smuggling with beefier law enforcement, but with mixed results. The RCMP has said that "there remains considerable ground to cover," whatever that vague admission means.

It is almost impossible to get an accurate or objective picture of the contraband cigarette problem. Huge bureaucracies, each with their own political agendas, toss figures around like tractors spreading fertilizer across a potato field. Numbers get sliced, diced, and manipulated to ensure they produce maximum effect in a world with limited attention. One of the most recent examples of this comes from the World Lung Foundation, where deft fingers manipulating calculators have produced the statistic that tobacco kills someone every six seconds.

One thing is certain: the Canadian tobacco taxation problems cover more ground than ever before. The problem of illicit tobacco was once restricted primarily to Ontario and Quebec, but it has now spread into other provinces. Seizures of contraband tobacco are fairly common in Atlantic Canada. Many are small, involving vans and pickup trucks travelling the main highways from Central Canada.

In the West illegal tobacco trade is increasing, and provincial governments there seem determined to fight the trade in court. A potentially major constitutional battle over Native tobacco is shaping up in the West.

Native manufactured tobacco, legal or illegal, was not common west of Ontario until recent years. Rainbow Tobacco Co. of Kahnawake began a western marketing campaign to convince western tribes of the economic benefits of selling cigarettes to their people. Rainbow's cigarettes are legally manufactured and licensed for sale on reserves. Rainbow contends that the federal Indian Act says the provinces cannot tax the personal property of a Native on a reserve, but at least one western province, Alberta, believes its tobacco taxes do apply to reserves. A legal battle has developed and will determine which side is right.

In 2011 Alberta seized sixteen million Rainbow Tobacco cigarettes from a Quonset hut on the Montana First Nation in Hobbema, Alberta. Robbie Dickson, chief executive officer of Rainbow, flew to Alberta to demand return of the cigarettes. Alberta refused and a constitutional law court fight has developed. Rainbow filed a $3.999 million lawsuit against Alberta. Natives have learned that one major benefit of tobacco money is that it allows them to afford to fight sovereignty issues in a justice system where no one gets anywhere without having big money.

The Montana First Nation seizure had a bizarre beginning. There had been a break-in and theft at the Quonset hut, so the band called the RCMP to investigate. When the RCMP and Alberta government saw the cigarettes, they seized them, even though they carried federal tax-paid stamps.

The fact that the cigarettes were seized on Native land just because they did not have provincial tax stamps, not required on Indian reserves, indicated that Alberta was deliberately looking for a court fight over Native tobacco. Rainbow products have also been seized in Manitoba, Saskatchewan, and British Columbia.

Dickson has shown he will take a strong stand against western seizures. He has met and received support from Native organizations in the West. The Assembly of First Nations passed a resolution in the summer of 2011 asking its national chief, Shawn Atleo, to push Ottawa and the provinces to back off provincial attempts to regulate tobacco trade between Native communities.

"Provincial governments have chosen to disregard and disrespect our inherent and Treaty rights by enacting legislation which attempts to regulate and limit our access to tobacco ... negatively impacting our ability to maintain our cultures and practices," said the resolution.

"It's not about tobacco anymore," Dickson told the *Kahnawake News*. "It's about Native sovereignty and our rights being stomped on."

Rainbow Tobacco products have also been seized by the Manitoba government, and one legal fight is even more complicated than at the Montana First Nation. Late in 2011 Manitoba law-enforcement officers seized ninety thousand cigarettes from the Dakota Chundee Smoke Shack near Pipestone, Manitoba. The packages carried Canada tax stamps, but no provincial stamps, and they were being sold outside reserve land. However, the Canupawakpa Dakota Nation argues that its treaty status is in question, leaving another fight for the courts to decide. Manitoba's cigarette tax is $45 a carton so huge amounts of money are involved.

The western confrontation looks similar to the legal warfare between some Iroquois tribes and the state of New York. Tribes like the Mohawks on the U.S. side of Akwesasne fought and lost court battles over New York's legal position that it has the right to tax brand-name cigarettes sold on reservations. At $4.35 per pack, the New York state tax is the highest in the United States.

The court losses led the Indians to open their own cigarette manufacturing plants. There are believed to be at least twelve Indian manufacturing plants in upper New York State, producing Native brands for sale to non-Natives through Native-owned convenience stores. The tribes argue they are sovereign nations and the cigarettes they make are exempt from state taxes. New York argues it has the right to tax any cigarettes sold to non-Natives, but has not done much to enforce that claim. When it does, there will no doubt be more protracted court fights.

It is now roughly thirty years since tobacco, which had been quietly declining in popularity with the general population, has drifted into the spotlight as a major taxation issue. The contraband trade continues to suck revenue out of government pockets, which are becoming increasingly less deep. Tax losses to outright smuggling, and to diversion based on sovereignty arguments, have become more significant during the current extended period of world financial problems. At the same time, governments around the world are cutting spending programs, some desperately, and are pursuing more revenue generation.

The 2012 Drummond Report on reforming Ontario government spending noted that with better enforcement, better education, and better relations with Native government, Ontario could increase tobacco revenue by $225 million a year. One of the first strategies the report suggests is discussion with Native governments on improving tobacco regulation on reserves. The Ontario auditor general has said that Ontario lost $500 million in 2006–07 to tobacco smuggling.

The pressure for governments to trim spending and plug revenue holes is everywhere. The Canadian Federal Strategic Operating Review plans to cut $4 billion a year in spending to 2014–15. Without action there are concerns about the sustainability of pensions and health care.

To make matters worse, some economists expect the world economic weakness will deteriorate further. A 2012 United Nations report says that world unemployment is too high, especially among young people, and is stalling economic recovery. It said that in 2011 there was a world employment deficit of sixty-four million jobs that needs to be eliminated.

All this makes for a world hungry for all the tax revenue it can get. The usual number given by various sources for lost tobacco tax revenue in Canada is $2.1 billion a year. In the United States, the estimate is $5 billion a year. In Germany the loss is €5.5 billion a year. Exact numbers are difficult to prove, and really don't matter. What is certain is that governments lose hundreds of millions of tobacco tax dollars every year. To add insult to injury, in their efforts to stanch the loss, they end up losing more, as the costs for law enforcement and the justice system continue to increase.

Calls for government action have become regular and can be expected to be louder and more frequent if economies continue to shrink. The tug-of-war continues between smoke-free world campaigners, who argue for higher taxes to reduce smoking, and policy makers who want lower taxes to reduce contraband's drain on tax revenues and law-enforcement resources. Tobacco control organizations argue that the gains made in reducing smoking rates already are slipping. Smoking rates, declining steadily since the 1960s, have flatlined. The federal tobacco control strategy had a goal of reducing the smoking rate, which was 19 percent in 2007, to 12 percent in 2011. The target wasn't met, and in 2011 the rate was somewhere between 17 and 21 percent.

Police efforts continue to be reinforced. In May 2010 a Combined Forces Special Enforcement Unit–Contraband Tobacco Initiative, led by the RCMP, was organized to coordinate federal, provincial, and municipal law-enforcement efforts against organized crime involved in contraband cigarette trade in the St. Lawrence River Valley.

Since then seizures have declined. RCMP seizures totalled 598,000 cartons/baggies in 2011. The volume of seizures was down in 2010 and 2011 from 2009, but was still higher than the 456,000 cartons seized in 1994 during the smuggling crisis. Seizures of fine-cut tobacco are the highest in history. They reached an all-time high of seventy thousand kilograms in 2008, then fell off to an average of thirty-five thousand kilograms a year in period 2009–11. More fine-cut seizures are related to more illegal manufacturing.

Whether declining seizures mean there is less contraband around, or whether the criminals are finding more secretive ways of moving it, is uncertain. It is known that smugglers are expert at changing the game. So much money is in play that they can afford the latest technology for monitoring law-enforcement moves. In 2012 a carton of legal cigarettes cost between $70 and $106 in Canada, depending on provincial or territorial tax rate. The black market sells the same amount of cigarettes in plastic bags for as low as $6 to $10.

Smugglers are once again using the waterways more. The thousands of nooks and crannies along the Canada-U.S. border area of the St. Lawrence make it impossible to find and stop all smugglers. The tricks of the contraband cigarette trade are seemingly endless, from aircraft surveillance to determine changes in police shifts, to the use of young female runners because the courts are less likely to send a woman to jail, especially if she has young children at home.

Smugglers find new holes; law enforcement works to plug them. It is a see-saw battle, seemingly never-ending. But too much harm is being inflicted on society for it not to end. Governments, and individuals, need to focus keenly on possible solutions, which surely exist for people determined to find them.

Tensions caused by the tobacco trade, and the gap in understanding between non-Natives and Natives, remain impediments to solutions. There is hope, however. As usual, it comes not from government initiatives broadcast loudly through advertisements and media releases. It comes from the small, little-publicized initiatives of individuals such as Francine Lemay.

Francine Lemay is the sister of the Quebec provincial police corporal shot and killed at Oka. Years after the shooting, Lemay attended a church gathering during which Mohawk women from Kanesatake had been invited to talk about their project of translating the Old Testament into Mohawk.

At the end of the presentation, Lemay stood and asked to speak. She told the assembly that she was the sister of the slain officer and asked the Mohawks for forgiveness for all the wrongs they had endured since the coming of the Europeans. She began to cry and so did the audience. Mavis Etienne, the Bible project coordinator and a Mohawk negotiator during the 1990 crisis, approached her and offered condolences, and an apology for not praying for the safety of the police that day.

For Lemay the events of that day marked the beginning of a special closeness with Kanesatake and a developing interest in a book called *At the Wood's Edge*, an anthology of the Kanesatake Mohawks. Lemay felt it was important that the information in the book be shared with the francophone community and decided to translate the book into French. The translation was published as *À l'Orée des Bois*.

Lemay attended Etienne's church in Kanesatake occasionally and was introduced there to Daniel Lacasse, who had been drawn to Kanesatake in a quest to build bridges. A couple of years later they were married. The best man at the wedding was Tracy Cross, brother of Ronald "Lasagna" Cross, one of the prominent warriors at the Oka confrontation.

Francine Lemay's story is one of hope for understanding between Natives and non-Natives, an understanding that might help in solving the contraband cigarette problems. It also offers a little hope for better media coverage of Native affairs. The Lemay story was brought forward by Loreen Pindera, CBC radio reporter and co-author of *The People of the Pines*, the definitive book about the Oka Crisis. It is a classic example of how reporters need to spend time getting to know the subjects they cover, and do detailed reporting instead of the quick-hit coverage that dominates the media today.

Intelligent and compassionate people taking intelligent and compassionate actions are important, but they alone will never solve the contraband cigarette problem. Finding solutions rests with the politicians, who regrettably are often not nearly as intelligent, nor as compassionate, as the people they serve.

Solutions are out there, waiting to be discovered. A strong willingness to search them out, along with an understanding of and willingness to resolve outstanding Native issues connected to them, are what's needed, and lacking now.

A paper written in the January 2011 edition of *Policy Options* placed the situation today in a succinct and clear paragraph. It was written by Tasha Kheiriddin, a writer, political commentator, and the former Quebec director of the Fraser Institute. "Since it is governments that both impose taxes and enforce the law, it is they that have the power to act to change this situation. They must weigh public health outcomes against the cost of criminal activity. It is not a politically palatable choice, for the reasons previously outlined, but it must be confronted. Allowing this situation to fester constitutes an abdication of the state's responsibility to its citizens."

23

Endgame

Talk of a world free of contraband, or even a smoke-free world, is a pipe dream: boastful talk bobbing aimlessly in oceans of words. Words cannot overcome the powerful forces driving the black-market tobacco trade. More police, more courts, more border restraints, even engaging the army, cannot eliminate tobacco smuggling. Only strong-willed action can.

There looms the roadblock. Governments are addicted to tobacco revenue. They cannot give it up. Some actually use tobacco revenue to balance their budgets. Programs and services would have to be jettisoned if tobacco tax revenue began to disappear. So, we have a situation in which government services rely on people continuing to smoke fully taxed cigarettes.

Some well-meaning anti-smoking groups object to describing governments as addicted to tobacco tax revenue. In fact, the Non-Smokers' Rights Association of Canada says that it is a myth perpetuated by the tobacco companies, and is inaccurate and dishonest. With all due respect to groups that do good work in reducing smoking rates, it is neither inaccurate, nor dishonest. There is plenty of evidence that governments are using most of the revenue for programs not related to stopping tobacco smuggling or helping people to quit the tobacco habit.

In June 2012 the U.S. Centers for Disease Control and Prevention reported that in the thirteen years ending 2010 U.S. state governments collected $244 billion in cigarette taxes and tobacco company settlement cash. However, the states appropriated only $8 billion for tobacco control programs, less than one-third of the $29 billion the CDC feels should have been spent.

That fact was likely a reason why, in June 2012, Californians rejected Proposition 29, which would have increased the state tax on cigarettes by $1 a pack to $1.87 per pack. It would have allowed equivalent tax increases on other tobacco products. That defeat showed that even though a large majority of people oppose smoking, they are fed up with governments blithely increasing taxes for one purpose, then redirecting the revenue for other purposes.

The magnificent contradiction is now annoyingly more difficult to overcome than it was for King James I and so many other leaders of government. French emperor Napoleon III would be amused to see the contradiction generating so much debate 150 years after he promised to ban tobacco — when and if someone could find a replacement that produced so much money for the state.

Tobacco control is an ugly balancing act for governments. It becomes uglier as the need for revenue grows, while the physical and social harms of smoking consume larger portions of national financial pies. In Canada the federal and provincial governments gathered $7.5 billion in tobacco tax revenues in 2010–11, and that's not counting provincial and federal sales taxes collected. The governments estimate they can get another $2 billion by eliminating the contraband trade, but have not made this an urgent priority at the highest political levels. That's because they will not commit themselves to finally resolving the connected Native issues.

In the meantime, what the public gets is more talk, fine-tuning of regulations, and more spending on law enforcement. Meanwhile, the contraband trade carries on, criminalizing many little people and providing experience and financial strength for major criminal gangs.

The voting public would likely support more action against contraband tobacco and even tighter controls on smoking. British surveys show that close to one-half of citizens would support an outright ban on tobacco sales. Eighty percent of Canadians don't smoke, and many of those who do wish they didn't, so it is possible that like the British, Canadians might support a ban on cigarette sales.

Many would support off-the-wall suggestions such as licensing smokers; scheduled, regular reductions in the amount of tobacco for sale, with prices rising as supplies dwindle; and making tobacco possession outside the home a criminal offence.

I am not advocating a tobacco ban or adoption any of the other radical ideas listed above. However, it is clear that large numbers of people would support a wide range of government actions against smoking and the trade in contraband tobacco.

It must be recognized, however, that many people wish to smoke. Without buyers, there would be no market, black, white, or otherwise. Buyers are a key to the contraband issue. The two best ways of dealing with them are through education and law enforcement. Unfortunately, many of the strategies used to both educate smokers and stem the illegal trade in tobacco have been ineffective.

The anti-smoking and tobacco control people could be doing much more, and differently, to resolve important tobacco problems. However, smoke from their passion to create a tobacco-free world sometimes gets in the eyes and obscures the big picture. Theirs obviously is important work, dedicated to creating a healthier society. Some of their messages, however, are so hyperbolic and exaggerated that they set eyes rolling and do little to reduce the number of smokers.

They tell us: someone dies in Ontario every forty minutes from tobacco; every cigarette you smoke takes seven minutes off your life; tobacco will kill one billion people this century, or one person every six seconds. People are expected to swallow these nuggets of information whole, like trusted medicine. Figures get tossed around like popcorn in a hot hopper, few persons, if any, ever checking their accuracy, or putting them into perspective.

People with lost limbs, tracheotomies, and paralysis are featured in the 2012 anti-smoking campaign launched by the Centers for Disease Control and Prevention and U.S. Department of Health. The campaign costs $54 million and hopes to get 50,000 Americans to stop smoking — $1,080 per convert.

Graphic, hard-hitting ads work, says CDC director Thomas R. Frieden. But you have to question his view, considering that scare tactics often don't work with addicted people. Surely our society is advanced enough that we don't need to show pictures of someone coughing up a black lung to educate people about the dangers of smoking.

Too many tobacco control bureaucracies get carried away, however, trying to bring more converts to their campaigns. Most of us already know that smoking causes serious health problems. The fact that X number of people die from smoking, or that treating smoking-related health issues costs us all X number of dollars stupidly simplifies the issues. Intelligent education that will help people understand the deeper issues is far more effective than campaigns of over-hyped messages.

Much of what is written about tobacco is embroidered to attract attention and to push readers onto a particular side of the many issues. The embroidery is not needed. It is a symptom of an illness in our society, where true information has been supplanted by over-hyped marketing intended to persuade, rather than to simply inform. Unembroidered facts are needed, not hype. The average person is quite capable of studying the facts and reaching his or her own conclusions about resolving tobacco issues.

Yes, smoking kills over time. So can a lot of other things, in some cases much more quickly. Nearly 3,500 people die on the world's roads every day, about 1.3 million a year. Tens of millions are injured every year; the costs to society are huge. I'd prefer to get one killer driver under control before taking a pack of untaxed cigarettes away from some underpaid factory worker.

Or, take the sugar out the cupboards of the so many millions of us who are overweight and creating a serious burden on health services. In 2012 University of California researchers published a study claiming that sugar contributes to thirty-five million deaths a year worldwide. The study said sugar is so dangerous it should be controlled through taxation and legislation. It suggests using taxation to double the price of fizzy drinks, restricting their sale to those over seventeen or eighteen, and tightening regulations covering school vending machines and snack bars.

Tobacco control groups need to find new ways of dealing compassionately and reasonably with the most addicted smokers. There are people, like Sigmund Freud, who find it impossible to beat the tobacco addiction no matter how hard they try. There are many, like Freud, who cannot quit even after being told they have cancer.

Smoking provides comfort for some less fortunate people. My grandmother, bedridden with crippling arthritis for eighteen years, began smoking in her sixties. It helped to relieve the pain, and the boredom of being in bed hour after hour.

Tobacco, after all, is not the only bad thing around but it seems to receive the most attention. Regretfully, some tobacco control work is typical bureaucratic make-work stuff, offering no new information, or new thinking. Consider this conclusion from the 2009 status report of the federal Task Force on Illicit Tobacco Products: "It is clear that there is no simple solution to the issue of contraband tobacco in Canada. It is equally clear that, moving forward, there are promising avenues to explore in close cooperation with our partners in affected First Nations communities, federal and provincial partners, the law-enforcement community as well as our partners in the United States.

"Addressing an issue as complex as contraband tobacco poses significant challenges...."

No kidding. A grade school kid given a couple of hours to research the subject could have come up with that.

Contrast that with a 2009 report on Commercial Tobacco in First Nations and Inuit Communities by the Non-Smokers' Rights Association/Smoking and Health Action Foundation. That document is clear, thoughtful, and hard hitting, without the hyperbole. It is helpful to anyone wanting information that can help them form ideas on the subject. It recommends seeking out a high-level envoy who can engage Native communities in discussions about tobacco. That's a genuine idea that the government should be considering.

People should not let bureaucracies do their thinking. The bureaucracies need to gather and present information that is as factual as possible, and from which we all can develop our own opinions. Of course the world would be healthier without commercial tobacco, but there are many side issues and ramifications that need to be thought through.

World smoking and tobacco smuggling have been around for five centuries now. To believe they can be made to disappear over the next couple of decades, without planning for possible consequences, is not realistic. The anti-smoking industry would be much more effective if it redirected some of its ample energy and resources toward full presentation of all the issues, consequences, and possible solutions.

There is progress in that direction. The Second U.S.-Canadian Bi-National Conference on the Illegal Tobacco Trade in 2011 included Native representation and made several specific and workable recommendations. It recommended political engagement involving the prime minister, the U.S. president, and First Nations leadership levels. It also recommended eliminating the international border through Akwesasne and working toward a National Native Free Trade Act.

Such discussions are only the beginning. There are many tobacco-related issues that need discussion and resolution, for instance the issues of freedom of choice and civil rights — issues about which Canadians are less passionate than their American neighbours. People have a right to smoke. Farmers have a right to grow tobacco. Companies have a right to manufacture tobacco products. None of these activities are against the law, provided restrictions found in smoking bylaws and company policies are observed. It's like alcohol use. It's legal and doesn't seriously injure society as long as the restrictions are followed.

If, however, tobacco use is discouraged and restricted, then society must deal with the enormous issue of how to plan to deal with the economic fallout of declining smoking rates. The World Bank has assumed that as more people stop smoking they will have more money to spend on other goods. It has also assumed that all the jobs lost in tobacco farming, processing, manufacturing, and distribution will be replaced by new jobs. That seems a bit of a stretch, reminiscent of the fiction told to Canadian tobacco farmers by their governments about the riches that were to be had if they shut their tobacco operations and grew soybeans, or some other crop. It sounded simple, but ask lifelong tobacco farmers just how difficult it has been.

Cigarettes are the world's most traded item and the tobacco business is one of the world's largest industries. The WHO estimates that the global tobacco market now is worth close to $500 billion a year. The International Labour Organization has estimated that

100 million people work in the world tobacco industry, including many thousands who work to eliminate smoking in the tobacco control industry. Tobacco taxes globally raise tens of billions of dollars that support myriad other jobs.

It's fine to say that people should not work in an industry that causes disease and premature death. However, tell that to a tobacco farm worker in Malawi who works dawn to dusk to feed his family. Or to a Native family on a Canadian reserve where tobacco has created the first steady income in generations.

The world economic benefits of tobacco cannot be ignored. Most of the shiny vehicles, new houses, recreation centres, and business offices seen on Indian territories in Canada and the United States were paid for by tobacco money.

As one Oneida leader in New York State recently told the *New York Times*: "We tried poverty for 200 years. We decided to try something different."

Unlike the rivers and creeks, however, tobacco revenue will not flow forever. In developed countries, where tobacco control has been most effective, tobacco jobs are becoming fewer. Workers used to making $50,000 year have lost their jobs and are either on social benefits or working in jobs that pay far less. The Bakery, Confectionery, Tobacco Workers and Grain Millers International Union in the United States has noted that in the past twenty years it has lost 30,000 members once employed in cigarette factories.

Smoking will decline throughout the world and the tobacco industry will produce fewer jobs, fewer economic benefits, and presumably fewer tax dollars. Overall, that is a good thing, but there is no evidence that governments are making any serious preparations to offset lost tobacco jobs and the decline of the tobacco industry economy in general.

A few years back, Juan Somavia, director-general of the International Labour Organization, warned that the future of people who rely on the industry must be considered: "Tobacco has never been more controversial than it is today. For many who work in the tobacco sector the world over, stagnating or declining employment is a burning workplace and social issue — especially among the most vulnerable such as migrants, women and children, ethnic minorities and castes or tribes who depend on tobacco for a livelihood. Their future must also be considered."

The poor, with their higher-than-average smoking rates, cannot be ignored. It is argued that high taxes force more of the poor to quit smoking, but it's an argument that does not fit with the facts. The same is true for the claim that education campaigns and cessation programs will solve the smoking problems of the poor. Anyone living at the poverty line and addicted to tobacco is going to be looking for the $5 man before reading government pamphlets about cessation programs or the evils of contraband.

Consideration of such consequences should be part of the tobacco control industry campaigns. Eliminating or dramatically reducing the contraband problem will hit hard at some segments of society. Just because it's illegal does not mean we should not be helping to soften the blow for those who get hurt.

Real help for poor smokers can come through directing more tobacco tax revenue toward them. When higher taxes impact the poor people addicted to tobacco, governments should consider compensating tax cuts on other necessities, such as food. Higher taxes can be an incentive for the poor to at least reduce consumption, but they are not the solution for eliminating smoking among the poor.

Some people argue that smoking hurts us all because of the huge health costs it incurs. That's a point that's easily put, but one that needs to be thought through and balanced. Smoking kills people at a younger age than might otherwise be expected. Those who die younger impose fewer of the burdens that most seniors generate for the health system. Also, smokers work all their lives contributing to pension funds, then die prematurely before they are able to collect the majority of their pensions, leaving more for the rest of us.

Easier to argue is removing smoking rights for youth. There are age laws for drinking and driving vehicles, and some people argue there should be for smoking. There are laws prohibiting the sale of tobacco to minors, and two provinces forbid youths from possessing tobacco.

A study released in October 2011 by the University of Florida and DePaul University in Chicago found that introducing youth possession laws for tobacco is an effective approach to reducing the number of young smokers. The study argues that if young people can't smoke openly because they're afraid of being ticketed by police, there's less peer pressure for others to pick up the habit.

The Canadian Convenience Stores Association (CCSA) agrees because current law puts the onus on the tobacco retailer, not the kids. The association has said the provinces should keep the laws making it illegal to sell tobacco to minors, but add new laws so enforcers can fine kids directly for smoking. Such a law would discourage smoking among the young people who currently bypass the stores to buy cigarettes on the black market.

There should also be a debate on whether the convenience stores should be allowed to sell tobacco, period. Perhaps tobacco should treated like alcohol: available only under government control, and sold only at government outlets. Give convenience stores the right to sell beer and wine in exchange for giving up tobacco sales.

The current situation in Ontario, where tobacco products are locked behind metal shutters, is an example of government and bureaucracy gone crazy.

There is the question, too, of whether the law should forbid possession of any black-market tobacco. For instance, if a police officer stops a car and sees a bottle of liquor on the front seat beside the driver, he or she will check to determine if the seal is broken. If there is a carton of cigarettes on the front seat, would it not make sense to determine if they carry the proper tax stamps? Ontario police recently received the power for plain-view seizures of illegal tobacco. Previously they had to receive Ministry of Finance permission to make such seizures. This idea is fraught with numerous problems, however, including the attitudes of police officers, who might feel they have more important things to do than to check for tax stamps on cigarettes.

The decision to increase police powers of search and seizure of tobacco creates the same situation as spending more money on law enforcement. Catch more tobacco smugglers who go to court, then ignore the fines and get back to smuggling. Or send them to jail where we spend more tax dollars keeping them.

Lowering tobacco taxes would reduce smuggling. That is a given. In the past, it has also been assumed that lowering tobacco taxes will increase, or at least stop, the decline of smoking rates. That assumption needs an accurate, unbiased relook. Is it true today that more people will smoke more cigarettes if taxes are lower? Perhaps, perhaps not. Can taxes be lowered to reduce contraband and at the same time institute programs that will help ensure a continuing decline in smoking?

There never has been in Canada a serious, targeted, effective campaign to recruit citizens in the war against contraband tobacco. Respect for government continues to decline, so anything the government says about smuggled tobacco hurting the country might only be greeted by smirks. However, in today's austere economic climate, perhaps the right messages might help, or perhaps even the right, non-preaching message delivered by private organizations.

Certainly more can be done to engage the United States, the source of huge numbers of cigarettes smuggled into Canada. There is a feeling that smuggling of tobacco from New York State into

Ontario and Quebec is not a big issue for the United States. It is for Canada, though, with law-enforcement agencies saying 90 percent of contraband cigarettes come from New York State.

People need to lean heavily on the politicians on both sides of the border, at the highest levels of Canadian, American, and Native governments, to ensure that they are working to make tobacco their number one priority.

Licensing of non-tobacco manufacturing materials such as cigarette paper, filters, and glue is an idea worth exploring. Jerry Montour, CEO of Grand River Enterprises, has said licensing these materials would make it more difficult for illegal manufacturers to obtain supplies. There are no restrictions on these materials, one reason being that some of them can be used in non-tobacco operations and licensing them could cause difficulties.

Our governments are paralyzed, however. They are stone edifices, incapable of the fresh thinking needed to solve the underlying issues. They have an attention deficit disorder, flitting from issue to issue like hummingbirds, too often putting political expediency ahead of the right thing to do. As a result, no real change occurs.

The danger of inaction lies not only in the increased crime brought by smuggling, or the revenue lost to governments. There is also a danger that the public will run out of patience and demand forceful actions based on incomplete knowledge of the situation, actions with implications that have not been fully thought through. Already there have been calls for raids to shut down tobacco factories considered illegal, all of which happen to be on Native lands.

Such raids would eliminate a chunk of the country's illegal cigarette trade, but they would also be unthinkably dangerous. Shutting the illegal factories could not be done without violence. More importantly, such raids would convey the message that Canadian governments have no interest in listening, negotiating, then acting to address Native concerns about how they are viewed and treated in this country.

When public patience wanes, politicians start gun-slinging and we end up with cave-dweller actions like Oka and Ipperwash.

The determination of many to eliminate smoking provides an opportunity for new thinking and new approaches, especially for improving the lives of Native peoples. The Native tobacco issue is inexorably tied to other longstanding Native issues. Native tobacco issues cannot be solved without attempting to solve these other issues.

The First Nations Tax Commission has said that it is ten times more difficult to create private wealth on reserves because of the federal Indian Act, and various land ownership restraints that apply to Native lands. Much First Nations land is undervalued, which results in fewer economic opportunities.

In the summer of 2011, National Chief Shawn Atleo called for repealing the Indian Act and the dismantling of the Indian Affairs Department, now renamed the Department of Aboriginal Affairs by the bureaucrats. That dismantling could be an important step in creating economic development opportunities that are more stable and more desirable than the tobacco trade.

The Indian Act, a combining of the Gradual Civilization Act and the Indian Enfranchisement Act in 1876, has regulated all facets of Indian life. Its purpose was to bring about assimilation, which it never achieved. It dictated who qualified as an Indian, how Indian bands would be run, who could vote in band elections. It destroyed the traditional roles of women and elders, who were removed from the official processes of governing bands.

The Indian Act's purpose supposedly was to protect the rights of Indians, but it imposed non-Native forms of living upon them and restricted their lives. It made them a federal responsibility, which led to residential schools where traditional customs and values were replaced by foreign values and morals.

Whenever abolition of the Indian Act is raised, there are cries of "What do you replace it with?" The answer to that is simple: Anything that removes the colonial yoke from First Peoples. The Indian Act is a colonial nightmare inflicted upon Native peoples and has done much to restrict their transition as a distinct society able to flourish within the larger society. The bureaucracy behind the Indian Act and the Department of Aboriginal Affairs is growing while some Native communities continue to struggle in living conditions unthinkable in any other part of Canadian society. The department employed 3,300 bureaucrats in the mid-1990s, and now is believed to employee 5,000 or more.

Natives receive needed help from this bureaucracy but their future growth is smothered by it. What's needed is the ability of Native people to deal with federal and provincial governments on a nation-to-nation basis. What we have now in many Native communities is false-front self rule in which bureaucrat puppeteers manipulate the strings to make the people dance.

Many Canadians favour a different contract with Native people, one that gives them full self-determination in their own territories and one that makes it easier for them to compete fairly in economic ventures. They've seen that the policies of past decades, with all their billions in taxpayer spending, do not work. It is time for bold moves. Government needs to hear the words of Native leaders like Atleo, and make negotiations for critical changes a standing priority.

It's not as if First Peoples have no history in markets and trading that create sustainable economies. They were trading long before we arrived, but because of European interference and domination were not able to develop legislative and administrative frameworks that support modern markets.

Native peoples began getting into commercial tobacco in recent years because it was much easier than trying to establish other businesses. It provided quick money that supported other business ventures.

Nobel prize-winning economist Douglass C. North has summed this up nicely: "The organizations that come into existence will reflect the opportunities provided by the institutional matrix. That is, if the institutional framework rewards piracy then piratical organizations will come into existence; and if the institutional framework rewards productive activities then organizations — firms — will come into existence to engage in productive activities."

Governments regularly give assistance to ventures such as the movie and auto industries. Yet for First Peoples serious about the tobacco industry there is resistance, and suspicions about contraband activities.

Compliant Native tobacco companies pay huge amounts of taxes, and receive nothing in return for their communities. It can be argued that Indian reserves already get plenty of financial aid; however, that's aid they would receive with or without a tobacco industry.

Native tobacco manufacturers like Grand River and Rainbow are restricted to supplying tobacco products to reserves, or in the Grand River case to buyers outside the country. Why would they not be allowed to compete with international companies like Imperial Tobacco and JTI Macdonald in selling cigarettes to non-Natives? Why not let them compete with the big boys and provide even more jobs on reserves?

Native people must be given an institutional framework that will allow positive and productive activities. That means ending centuries-old colonial attitudes toward them and allowing them unqualified self-determination.

Natives should also be helped to realize more of the benefits of the tobacco industry by allowing them to collect tobacco taxes, so long as they account for them and use the money to create other more desirable and long-lasting businesses. This is being done in parts of Canada and the United States. The administration of Native affairs is a crazy quilt, however. A piece of the picture here, another piece there. Thousands of bureaucrats busy with needles and threads, but no one knowing what the pattern should be.

On some reserves in eastern Canada and British Columbia, tobacco sellers collect provincial and federal taxes, which are returned to band councils for community use.

In other provinces, notably Ontario, tobacco sold on reserves is exempt from taxes but there are regulations allocating so much tobacco to each reserve. Some of the allocations are bizarre, allowing hundreds of cigarettes per day for each man, woman, and child.

Quebec tries to collect provincial tax on tobacco sold by Natives to non-Natives, then transfers it back to the Native governments. There is a similar process in New Brunswick.

Compounding this diversity of regulations is a lack of agreement throughout Indian nations on some important issues, tobacco in particular. Some see commercial tobacco as critical for economic development. Others see it as a sacrilegious use of a sacred item. Still others do not favour the Native tobacco industry but see it as a powerful sovereign rights lever. Native police forces at places like Six Nations, Kahnawake, and Akwesasne refuse to be involved in tobacco enforcement because of the sovereignty issues.

More First Nations are developing strong economic bases, and in most cases these are the result of strong tribal governance anchored in tribal culture. A business culture that takes advantage of traditional values. Studies have found that the most successful Native business ventures are collectively owned. There are stakeholders instead of shareholders and the business reflects the desires of the community.

That requires strong leadership, which sometimes comes naturally, but more often is developed. Strong leadership keeps tribal politics from interfering with the business development. Too often business start-ups in Native communities become social handouts because people are so anxious for immediate work that no thought is given to the longer term.

The Native tobacco industry has become more than an economic quick hit. The factories and smoke shacks are providing steady jobs and stability on some reserves. They also have brought problems in the form of outside criminal organizations, and tensions over traditional versus non-traditional beliefs. Many people on the outside of Native communities see the industry as shady or outright illegal.

What's needed is normalization in which Native industry competes on a fair and equal footing on and off reserves. Normalization includes revenue-sharing agreements in which Native communities benefit from tobacco sales the way the rest of the country does. Whether we like it or not, smoking pays for some of the benefits citizens receive in health, education, and other government services.

There can be no end-game for contraband tobacco until related Native issues are addressed. That requires a fresh mindset in which we give up trying to solve the problems with police actions. Police actions are part of the age-old, colonial mentality that sees Indians as a threat and guns as a solution.

Our society needs to stop laying the contraband stigma on all Native tobacco. Legally produced Native cigarettes aren't any different than the ones produced by Big Tobacco. They are not good for you, but some people are addicted to them and they pay a good-size chunk of society's bills.

Contraband tobacco is one issue. Normalizing legal Native tobacco is another, and will require clear thinking, free of the stereotyping and outright racism of the past. Some people believe we have made marvellous progress in ending the stereotyping of First Peoples. However, there is much evidence that intolerance and racism against Native people still exists, openly and in the hearts of too many people.

The imperative for an end-game is a blueprint managed by a brilliant, decisive, and passionate person or persons who can draw together all the stakeholders to debate, negotiate, and make the difficult decisions needed to set up an end-game. The blueprint must contain a no-turning-back plan to settle the Native issues enmeshed in the overall tobacco problem. These include sovereignty, economic development, and governance: in general, finally reaching some way of helping Native people to live comfortably with their culture and their heritage inside our society.

This will require something rarely seen on a national scale in Canada — a tightly focused, non-political, passionate drive that declares: no matter how complicated or difficult, this will be achieved. Canadians saw this in the late 1970s when Terry Fox, a one-legged kid from British Columbia, decided to fight cancer by running coast to coast. Setting up the end-game for contraband tobacco, while finally settling five hundred years of Native issues, should be a national dream — one that is achievable. It should be the dream of the Prime Minister's Office.

The positive side of the world tobacco situation is that there is time to work out solutions for the problems that will occur as tobacco use declines. It will be many decades, if it ever happens, before smoking is eliminated. There is time for policymakers to develop strategies for replacing the millions of jobs that will be lost and to make up for the lost economic benefits of tobacco.

There is not a lot of time left, however, to resolve Native issues. Too many government policies have failed. The Native people wear the failures like a stigma. The more negative news our society receives about Natives, the closer we come to throwing up our hands and saying: "It's impossible. We've tried everything. Nothing ever will work."

That should never happen. Canada is a rich and compassionate country known for its fairness in understanding other people's problems. It has an opportunity to solve this one and to stand taller in the eyes of the world.

For their part, Native people will continue to survive and progress in the North American society and culture created by the Europeans. Many will continue to suffer the consequences of the economic disadvantage, but Native thought and Native culture will not go away as the colonials had wished.

One wonders how the story of North America would have been different had Columbus accepted the tobacco in the spirit it was offered. The evolution of the recreational use of tobacco, and its inherent problems, would likely have been the same, but Indian life might have been much different.

The tobacco leaves offered to Columbus were a gift, showing respect, and that gift required that respect be shown in return. Had the Europeans accepted and respected Indian civilization, cultures, and traditions, there might have developed a partnership for building a New World society. The lack of respect for what the Europeans considered a savage society became the foundation for centuries of social problems that continue to exist today.

Indian societies now are taking back the tobacco offered to Columbus in 1492. It is not just a reclaiming of the chemical-laced tobacco rolled into white tubes that fills the marketplace today. It is a reclaiming of the sacred tobacco with the spiritual connections that the European colonists chose to ignore.

Appendix:
Charts

Chart 1: Cigarette Prices in Canada.

This chart shows that a carton of two hundred cigarettes cost more than $100 in four Canadian provincial or territorial jurisdictions. Quebec had the lowest average price at $72.75 per carton, while the Northwest Territories had the highest at $113.39. The prices shown were accurate as of April 24, 2012, but change frequently.

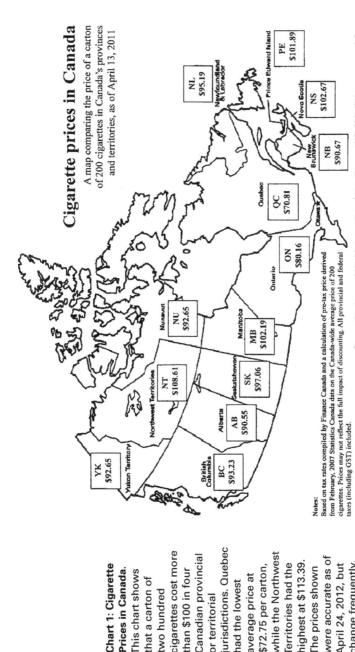

Cigarette prices in Canada

A map comparing the price of a carton of 200 cigarettes in Canada's provinces and territories, as of April 13, 2011

YK $92.65 — Yukon Territory

NT $108.61 — Northwest Territories

NU $92.65 — Nunavut

BC $93.23 — British Columbia

AB $90.55 — Alberta

SK $97.06 — Saskatchewan

MB $102.19 — Manitoba

ON $80.16 — Ontario

QC $70.81 — Quebec

NL $95.19 — Newfoundland & Labrador

PE $101.89 — Prince Edward Island

NS $102.67 — Nova Scotia

NB $90.67 — New Brunswick

Ottawa

Notes:
Based on tax rates compiled by Finance Canada and a calculation of pre-tax price derived from February, 2007 Statistics Canada data on the Canada-wide average price of 200 cigarettes. Prices may not reflect the full impact of discounting. All provincial and federal taxes (including GST) included.

Source: Smoking and Health Action Foundation, Ottawa, (613) 230-4211, www.nsra-adnf.ca

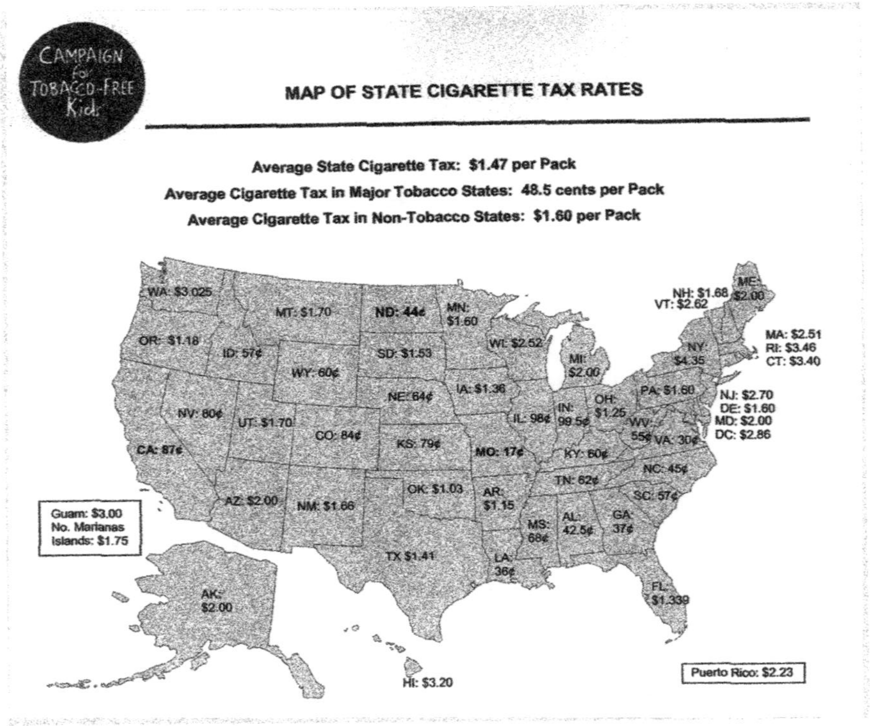

MAP OF STATE CIGARETTE TAX RATES

Average State Cigarette Tax: $1.47 per Pack

Average Cigarette Tax in Major Tobacco States: 48.5 cents per Pack

Average Cigarette Tax in Non-Tobacco States: $1.60 per Pack

Chart 2: U.S. State Cigarette Tax Rates. Cigarette tax rates vary wildly in the United States. In New York State the tax was $4.35 per pack of twenty cigarettes in 2012. In Virginia the tax was only thirty cents per pack. Differing state tax rates make it profitable for smugglers to move cigarettes across state lines.

Courtesy Campaign for Tobacco Free Kids

Canadian Tobacco Tax Revenues 2006 - 2011

	2006-2007	2007-2008	2008-2009	2009-2010	2010-2011
Newfoundland	110,000,000	107,758,000	111,953,000	113,000,000	135,000,000
Prince Edward Island	24,265,000	23,931,000	27,867,600	31,000,000	33,200,000
Nova Scotia	145,091,000	145,573,000	147,654,000	199,149,000	211,856,000
New Brunswick	81,900,000	79,900,000	103,700,000	102,600,000	126,800,000
Quebec	678,439,000	646,819,000	593,735,000	663,470,000	764,239,000
Ontario	1,236,000,000	1,127,000,000	1,044,000,000	1,083,000,000	1,160,000,000
Manitoba	201,576,342	190,627,400	189,632,718	215,500,000	233,700,000
Saskatchewan	150,776,000	190,412,000	199,072,000	196,868,000	235,100,000
Alberta	780,000,000	845,000,000	828,000,000	864,000,000	893,000,000
British Columbia	726,000,000	692,000,000	708,000,000	682,000,000	734,000,000
Provincial Total	4,134,047,342	4,140,062,400	3,953,614,318	4,150,587,000	4,526,895,000
Canada Total	2,492,359,786	2,663,914,023	2,530,655,522	2,629,538,912	3,011,472,182
Federal- Provincial Total	6,626,407,128	6,969,076,939	6,484,269,840	6,780,125,912	7,538,367.18
Change	-5.9	1.9	-3.4	4.6	11.2

Chart 3: Canadian Tobacco Tax Revenues. Canadian governments took in $7.5 billion in tobacco tax revenue in the fiscal year 2010–11. This was an increase of almost 7 percent over the previous year. The totals do not include sales taxes on tobacco products. This chart is compiled from information gathered from various sources.

Canadian Smokers by Province 2008

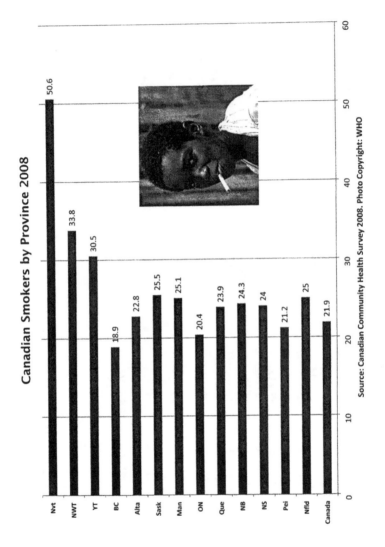

Province	Value
Nvt	50.6
NWT	33.8
YT	30.5
BC	18.9
Alta	22.8
Sask	25.5
Man	25.1
ON	20.4
Que	23.9
NB	24.3
NS	24
Pei	21.2
Nfld	25
Canada	21.9

Source: Canadian Community Health Survey 2008. Photo Copyright: WHO

Chart 4: Canadian Smokers by Province. Canadian smoking rates are highest in the three northern territories. The Canadian average is 21.9 percent.

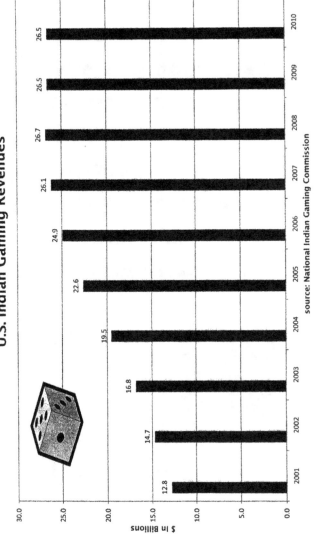

U.S. Indian Gaming Revenues

source: National Indian Gaming Commission

Chart 5: U.S. Indian Gaming Revenues. Revenues from gaming on U.S. Native American reserves have risen dramatically in the past decade. There are signs, however, that they are beginning to decline.

Rate of Youth Jailed

■ Aboriginal ■ Non-Aboriginal

Chart 6: Rate of Canadian Youth Jailed. Almost one-quarter of all Canadians jailed are Natives, even though they make up only 3 percent of the population. Rates of Native jailings in Canada smack of racism and have been called a national disgrace by various groups and institutions, including Corrections Canada. This chart is compiled from information collected from Statistics Canada and other government agencies.

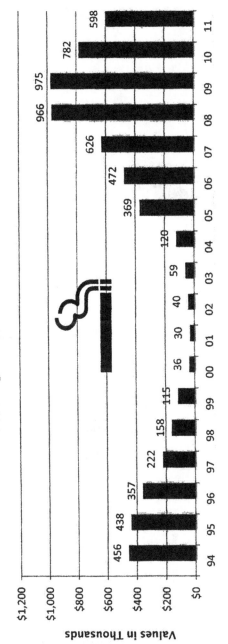

RCMP Cigarette Seizures 1994 to 2011

Chart 7: RCMP Cigarette Seizures. Contraband cigarette seizures by the Royal Canadian Mounted Police have increased steadily during the past decade. The increased number of seizures reflects tougher enforcement but also could be the result of increasing smuggling activity.

Source: RCMP

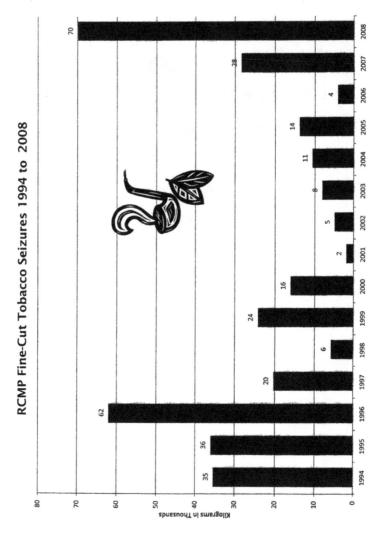

RCMP Fine-Cut Tobacco Seizures 1994 to 2008

Kilograms in Thousands

Year	Value
1994	35
1995	36
1996	62
1997	20
1998	6
1999	24
2000	16
2001	2
2002	5
2003	8
2004	11
2005	14
2006	4
2007	28
2008	70

Chart 8: RCMP Fine-Cut Tobacco Seizures. Seizures of bulk fine-cut tobacco can reflect an increase in illegal cigarette production for the contraband market. Seizure numbers have been relatively high in the past five years, following an upward trend in tobacco taxation.

Source: RCMP

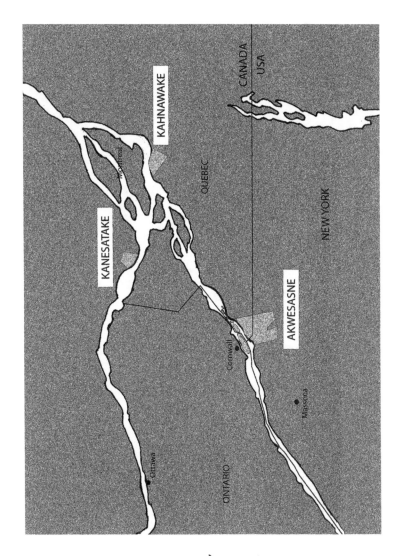

Chart 9: St. Lawrence River Map. The fight for sovereignty and the tobacco trade have caused much upheaval at the Mohawk reserves of Akwesasne, Kanesatake, and Kahnawake.

Akwesasne lands are located on the Canada-U.S. border, and tribal governments must deal with two different federal governments, plus the provincial or state governments of Ontario, Quebec, and New York.

Map by Dan Pantaleo

Further Reading of Interest on Tobacco and Native Life

Bearman, Peter, Kathryn M. Neckerman, and Leslie Wright, eds. *After Tobacco: What Would Happen If Americans Stopped Smoking*. New York: Columbia University Press, 2011.

Bolton, Herbert Eugene, and Thomas Maitland Marshall. *The Colonization of North America, 1492–1783*. New York: Macmillan Company, 1922.

Brandt, Allan M. *The Cigarette Century: The Rise, Fall, and Deadly Persistence of the Product That Defined America*. New York: Basic Books, 2007.

Cartier, Jacques. *Bref récit et succincte narration de la navigation faite en MDXXXV et MDXXXVI par le capitaine Jacque Cartier, aux îles de Canada, Hochelaga, Saguenay et autres*. *www. gutenberg.org/files/12356/12356-h/12356-h.htm*.

———. *The Voyages of Jacques Cartier*. Ed. Ramsay Cook. Toronto: University of Toronto Press, 1993.

Casas, Bartolomé de las. *An Account, Much Abbreviated, of the Destruction of the Indies*. Trans. Andrew Hurley. Ed. Franklin W. Knight. Indianapolis, IN: Hackett Publishing Co. Inc., 2003.

Columbus, Christopher. *The Journal of Christopher Columbus (During His First Voyage, 1492–93) and Documents Relating the Voyages of John Cabot and Gaspar Corte Real*. Ed. Clements

R. Markham. Cambridge, MA: Cambridge University Press, 2010.

Fagan, Brian M. *The Great Journey: The Peopling of Ancient America.* London: Thames and Hudson Ltd., 1987.

Johansen, Bruce Elliot, and Barbara Alice Mann, eds. "Iroquois Confederacy," in *The Encyclopedia of the Haudenosaunee.* Santa Barbara, CA: Greenwood Publishing Group, 2000.

Latimer, Jon. *Buccaneers of the Caribbean: How Piracy Forged an Empire.* London: Weidenfeld & Nicolson, 2009.

Morison, Samuel Eliot. *Samuel de Champlain: Father of New France.* Boston: Little, Brown and Company, 1972.

Proctor, Robert N. *The Nazi War on Cancer.* Princeton, NJ: Princeton University Press, 2000.

Rabushka, Alvin. *A Brief History of the Regulation and Taxation of Tobacco in England.* Princeton, NJ: Princeton University Press, 2008.

Stuart, James (King). *A Counter-Blaste to Tobacco. www.laits.utexas. edu/poltheory/james/blaste.*

Winter, Joseph C., ed. *Tobacco Use by Native Americans: Sacred Smoke and Silent Killer.* Norman, OK: University of Oklahoma Press, 2000.

Index

Page numbers in italics refer to images and their captions.

ALSO BY JIM POLING, SR.

Waking Nanabijou
Uncovering a Secret Past
978–1550027570
$26.99

Jim Poling, Sr., takes on the most important assignment of his career when he investigates his mother's past and stumbles upon a mystery that reveals the destructive force of discrimination in the history of Canadian Aboriginal relations. A search that begins in anger at his mother's secrecy concludes with an understanding of her actions. In the process Poling explores the place of families within Canadian society and uncovers the shameful ongoing prejudice against Native Peoples and the abusive treatment of illegitimacy.

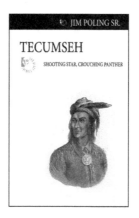

Tecumseh
Shooting Star, Crouching Panther
978–1554884148
$19.99

Shawnee war chief Tecumseh was a great leader who dedicated his life to stopping American expansion and preserving the lands and cultures of North American Aboriginal peoples. Although he perished during a final standoff with American forces at the Battle of Moraviantown, Tecumseh left an indelible mark on the history of both Canada and the United States. Tellingly, one of the greatest tributes to Tecumseh came from his enemy, William Henry Harrison, who later became the president of the United States. He called Tecumseh an "uncommon genius," who in another place, another time, could have built an empire.

DUNDURN
www.dundurn.com

Visit us at
Dundurn.com
Definingcanada.ca
@dundurnpress
Facebook.com/dundurnpress